Learn
BASIC
LIBRARY
SKILLS

Helen Rowe
Trina Grover

TotalRecall Publications, Inc.
1103 Middlecreek
Friendswood, Texas 77546
281-992-3131   281-482-5390 Fax
www.totalrecallpress.com

Copyright © 2015 Helen Rowe and Trina Grover
Based on the original work by Elaine Anderson, Mary Gosling,
Mary Mortimer, Mary McConnell and Trina Grover

ISBN: 978-1-59095-434-8
UPC: 6-43977-44343-4

Printed in the United States of America with simultaneous
printing in Australia, Canada, and United Kingdom.

FIRST INTERNATIONAL EDITION, MARCH 2015
1   2   3   4   5   6   7   8   9   10

TABLE OF CONTENTS

ACKNOWLEDGEMENTS

Thanks to Mary Mortimer, Mary Gosling, Elaine Anderson and Mary McConnell who wrote the previous editions of *Learn basic library skills*, and who kindly allowed their text to form the basis of this international edition.

Many thanks to our colleagues at Ryerson University in Canada and our colleagues in Australia. We also thank our students for asking the questions to which this book provides the answers.

INTRODUCTION

This book covers the skills needed when beginning work in a library or other information agency. The book describes tasks usually allotted to staff who begin in clerical, temporary, casual and volunteer positions, library trainees, aspiring library technicians and librarians starting their training, and others who find themselves working in a library or similar information agency with no relevant training or experience.

The book is designed for use on your own or in a formal course of study.

Each chapter deals with a section of basic library work, and the knowledge and skills needed to perform it well. The more you understand the tasks and procedures and the reasons for them, the more competently you will carry them out.

Where standard rules exist (e.g., filing rules), they are included. For procedures which vary from library to library, we outline a reasonably common approach (or two), or encourage you to find out how it is done in a library you know.

Throughout the book you will find exercises to practice and test your skills and quizzes to test your understanding. There are answers for self-checking at the back of the book. You may not always agree completely with the answers given, and it will be useful to check them with an instructor or experienced librarian.

Note on Spelling and Capitalization

This edition is designed for use in North America, Europe and Australasia, across countries that employ different spelling conventions for English words. For consistency, American spelling has been adopted for the text.

Titles included in the text are capitalized according to standard library cataloging practice — that is, apart from names, only the first word of the title has a capital letter. This is intended to accustom library students and staff to this style.

CHAPTER ONE
Basic Library Skills

Introduction

Library skills are essential in libraries. However, they can be used in a wide variety of other institutions including information centers, research hubs, museums and archival organizations. Staff in each of these institutions need library skills to help them:

- understand information
- purchase resources
- organize collections
- manage and present information
- deal with clients.

Libraries endeavor to connect people with the information they want. To achieve this, library staff need:

- reliable and consistent access to information
- technical skills to organize and access the information
- communication skills to help patrons use the information.

This chapter provides an overview of what happens in libraries. It introduces readers to categories of library material, basic library organization, and the skills required to work in the library environment. Each of the points discussed here will be covered in more depth in later chapters.

Access to Information

Traditionally, libraries physically collected information in printed and other formats, and housed it in their library building.

Libraries now provide access to information for their clients in other ways as well, using, among other things, databases, online services, and shared networks. These resources are created and stored elsewhere, outside the library, but clients are able to link in to them to find the information they require.

Types of Library Material

Content collected by libraries may be in the form of text, music, statistics, visual or audio, and then packaged in different physical formats such as printed pages or digital files on a disc or online. Most users are not concerned about the format in which information is presented, provided they can easily find a copy to borrow or use. Sometimes, however, the format is just as important as the content. For example, someone travelling long distances in a car cannot make good use of a printed book, but an audio book would meet their need.

Types of Content Collected by Libraries

form of content	analog examples	digital examples
text	printed books & magazines microforms	e-books & e-serials
spoken word	books on (magnetic cassette) tape	audio books on CD, streamed audio files
cartographic	printed maps	Google maps
moving images	films on VHS	DVDs, streamed videos
notated music	printed scores	digital sheet music
performed music	magnetic cassette tapes	CDs, streamed music files
still image	photographs on paper	digital photographs

Libraries usually group materials into a number of categories to manage them more easily. Common categories are electronic information, print materials and non-print materials.

Electronic Information
With the increase in resources obtainable via the Internet, much more of the information that libraries can offer to their clients is available in an electronic form. These resources are accessible using a computer but are not physically stored in the library.

This is beneficial to users as information is provided:
- faster
- at any time (not just when the library is open)
- more conveniently, as access to resources may be available from home or in the library or anywhere else by means of a computer.

There are benefits for libraries as well because these resources:
- don't take up valuable space on library shelves
- can't be stolen or destroyed
- depending on the license agreement, allow more than one user to access information at the same time.

Electronic resources are available in many different file formats and sizes. They are often presented as part of a web page (a document that can be read by a browser) or a web site (a collection of related web pages designed to be used together). Examples include:
streaming media: video or audio content sent in compressed form over the Internet and played immediately, rather than being saved to the hard drive. (The verb 'to stream' refers to the process of delivering media in this manner; the term refers to the delivery method of the medium rather than the medium itself).

e-journals: periodical publications published in electronic format, usually on the Internet. Also known as electronic journals, ejournals, and electronic serials.

e-books: book-length publications in digital form, consisting of text, images, or both, readable on computers or other electronic devices. Also known as electronic books, eBooks, e-Books, ebooks, digital books, and e-editions.

online databases: data structures that store organized information. Some databases contain the whole text of articles, or even complete books, which can be read online or printed. Other databases provide only basic citation information about the item – e.g., author, title of article, title of journal, issue of journal etc. Clients use this information to find the item in the library's collection, in another library, or via a computer.

Print Materials
Monographs
Monograph means 'produced once' and is derived from *mono* (Latin for *one*) and *graph* (Greek for *write*). The term is used to distinguish items issued once (also known as books) from those continuously issued (serials).

Print monographs include:
printed books: sheets of paper generally printed on both sides, folded and sewn, glued or spiral bound, enclosed in a cover.

manuscripts: usually on paper, written by hand (e.g., drafts of novels or poems).

pamphlets: unbound works of less than 50 pages.

ephemera: printed material intended to have a short life (e.g., leaflets, sale catalogs, political pamphlets, menus, theater programs).

newspaper clippings: news items, articles etc., cut from newspapers, indexed and filed.

Serials
Print serials are also called periodicals. They include journals, magazines, newspapers and annuals. These are publications that are issued at regular or irregular intervals, have a common title, and are intended to continue for an indefinite period of time.

Monographs in Series
Some monographs are published as part of a series. Most libraries treat these as monographs, acquiring and cataloging each item separately as it arrives. Some libraries, however, purchase every title in a series and arrange with the vendor to ensure that each title is forwarded to the library when it is published. These books are bought, processed and recorded within the serials subsystem by serials staff. This arrangement is often referred to as a **standing order**.

Non-Print Materials
This category is also referred to as non-book material. It consists of materials that are not primarily printed text and may require equipment in order to view it. The procedures for ordering and receiving this type of material often match those used to acquire print monographs and serials, but it is common practice to subdivide these resources into smaller categories that share similar physical characteristics.

Non-print materials include:

maps, plans, diagrams: large sheets, usually of paper or card stock, with cartographic or diagrammatic information; generally intended to be folded, rolled or hung.

pictures: single sheets on which pictorial information is displayed (e.g., drawings, paintings, prints, photographs).

films and slides: photographic images developed frame by frame onto a continuous strip of cellulose.

videotapes: magnetic tapes with visual and audio recording.

sound recordings: any format of recorded sound, including mp3s, compact discs, audiobooks, audiocassettes and vinyl records.

computer software: machine-readable instructions stored on CD-ROMs, DVDs and online; must be accessed and used by computer.

microform: documents reproduced in miniature for economy of storage and weight; read by projecting the enlarged image onto a screen (e.g., microfilm, microfiche).

artefacts, realia: real, hand-made, or machine-made three-dimensional objects including dioramas, games, models, specimens.

Basic Organization of a Library

Libraries are organized to store information so that clients and staff can retrieve it in the most effective manner. There are, however, many variations in how libraries organize their staff to carry out this goal. In this introduction we describe the most traditional functional design of a library staff structure. (For a discussion of this and other structures, see Chapter 4 of *Learn library management* by Jacinta Ganendran, from which the diagram on the next page is adapted.)

Functional Design

This structure usually consists of a number of sections or departments which deal with library materials and services. Although the diagram here includes the functions of administration and information technology, the descriptions that follow focus on the sections of technical services and public (also known as client or reader) services.

```
                        ┌─────────────────────┐
                        │   LIBRARY MANAGER   │
                        └─────────────────────┘
```

INFORMATION TECHNOLOGY	TECHNICAL SERVICES	ADMINIS-TRATION	PUBLIC SERVICES

ACQUISITIONS	CATALOGING	CIRCULATION	REFERENCE

The diagram shows that technical services staff acquire and organize material. Their responsibilities include receiving and processing the material (e.g., acquisitions, cataloging, and collection maintenance). In large libraries, this may be broken down further with individual sections dealing with particular formats of material (e.g., serials or music).

In contrast, public services (sometimes known as client services or reader services) deal with clients face-to-face. These services include borrowing and returning materials, shelving, answering users' enquiries, and reader education.

Each of these two sections has its own set of tasks that require particular knowledge and skills, but they also need to communicate effectively with each other and with the other sections of the library.

Work Flow
The diagram on the next page illustrates a typical work flow in a library. It is followed by a brief description of the work carried out in each section of a library.

Flow of Material Through a Library

TECHNICAL SERVICES
ACQUISITIONS

Purchase request received from client or collection development section

↓

Details verified

↓

Order or subscription prepared and sent to preferred vendor

↓

Details placed in 'on order file'

↓

Ordered item arrives from vendor

↓

Item matched against order record

↓

Invoice sent to account section

↓

Details placed in 'in process file'

↓

Item accessioned:
- ownership stamp
- date stamp
- barcode
- issue of print serial recorded

↓

CATALOGING

Item cataloged:
- copy cataloging or
- original cataloging
    - descriptive cataloging
    - subject headings
    - classification

↓

FINAL PROCESSING

Item processed for use:
- tattle tape
- spine label
- covering and/or reinforcing
- special symbols indicating location, format or loan period

↓

PUBLIC SERVICES

Item to Public Services for:
- circulation
- shelving
- promotion and display
- reference and current awareness services
- reader education

↓

COLLECTION
MAINTENANCE

Ongoing collection maintenance, either in Technical Services or Public Services:
- shelving and shelf-reading
- repair
- inventory
- weeding
- disposal
- binding

Technical Services
Acquisitions

Acquisitions staff obtain new material for the library's collection. Tasks include ordering, receiving, checking that incoming materials match the order, arranging for payment, marking the library's ownership, and recording receipt of all new library material. It may also include receiving (sometimes even soliciting) gifts and exchanges, and deciding how to handle them. The financial responsibility requires keeping track of the library's spending in relation to the library budget and knowing how much funding remains, ensuring that the library is within its budget allocation.

Cataloging

This section maintains **bibliographic control** of the library's collection. That is, the staff produce records that describe items, assign classification numbers and subject headings, and record these details in the catalog and in authority files.

The preliminary work of this section requires searching the library's (and other) catalogs and databases, to find existing records for the items, or records that may assist the library staff in creating original records.

Final Processing

This process is also known as 'end processing'. After items have been cataloged, they are prepared for loan and/or use in the library. This involves labeling, where the call number is placed on the spine of each book or indicated clearly on other types of material. Some libraries cover and/or otherwise strengthen books to prolong their lives. Non-book material is packaged so that it can be shelved and borrowed easily. Security (e.g., tattle tape) is added at this stage.

Public Services
Circulation

The lending and returning of library materials are key services. In order to do this correctly, staff must understand the intricacies of the circulation system. As this is the key point of access for library clients, it is essential that staff know how to deal with clients, especially clients who may be impatient or dissatisfied with the service.

Shelving

Items must be shelved correctly, so that clients can find them - they are shelved when first ready for use, and after each use. Staff should check shelves regularly, using a shelf reading schedule, to ensure that items have been replaced accurately.

Promotion and Display

It is important for the library to promote its services to all of its potential clients, so that the library is regularly used and its value is appreciated. Promotional activities could range from running an art competition during Book Week to offering specialized current awareness programs within an organization; from displaying new acquisitions on shelves in the library foyer to emailing individual clients to notify them of items of particular interest.

Reference Service

Reference services vary considerably among libraries, depending on the nature and purpose of the library and the level of staff assigned to this section. For example, in a corporate or legislative library, services can include providing answers to specific questions, performing extensive searches, and recording the results. In a public or school library, services could focus on maintaining a good reference collection and assisting clients to find the information for themselves.

Reader Education

Libraries are used more effectively by clients who understand how the library is organized and how to search the catalog and other databases. Staff can provide assistance ranging from one-on-one instruction to teaching groups how to use the catalog efficiently, find answers to specific questions, search for information on the Internet, and so on.

As more information is retrieved electronically, it becomes increasingly important to teach clients to define their information needs, to identify the most likely sources, and to evaluate their results.

It is vital for library staff to 'value-add' to sources of information such as the Internet, CD-ROMs, and so forth, so that clients benefit from their information retrieval skills. In value-adding, library staff may help someone assess which is the most significant information retrieved, or they may limit the number of items retrieved online to the most relevant, or use other methods to find the specific information a client requires. Unless library staff promote their skills in these areas, the community may conclude that libraries and their specialist staff are no longer relevant to the process of obtaining information.

Collection Maintenance

This encompasses all activities involved in keeping the collection current, attractive and easy to use. Activities include shelving and shelf-reading, repair of damaged items, inventory (also known as stocktaking) and weeding. Public services staff perform several of the tasks, technical services staff are responsible for others, and both sections may work together on some of these activities.

EXERCISE 1.1

Indicate which library section or department (i.e. Technical Services or Public Services) would be most likely to do the tasks listed in the table below. More than one task may be associated with each work area.

Library Task	Library Department
Shelving	
Promotion and Display	
Circulation	
Reader Education	
Acquisitions	
Cataloging	
Reference Service	
Final Processing	
Collection Maintenance	

Technical Skills

Technical skills are needed to organize library material. Accuracy and attention to detail are the basis of strong technical skills in library work.

Libraries, even small ones, store a great deal of material and staff need to be able to find items quickly. This requires creating consistent records and maintaining them accurately to prevent problems which could be easily avoided. Such problems could be:

- the incorrect spelling of an author's name in the catalog record prevents a book from being found easily
- clients are irritated if they receive overdue notices because returned items were not properly checked in
- hours can be wasted searching for a 'missing' issue of a serial that has been shelved in the wrong place.

Over the years, libraries have developed rules and procedures to streamline their work and provide a reliable information environment of benefit to both library staff and clients. Libraries are able to share the bibliographic records they create online, which reduces the amount of cataloging each library needs to do individually. With improved telecommunications, clients can access information stored in remote locations. These added benefits demand that the procedures for recording and storing information provide consistency. Only then will the processes become simpler rather than more complex.

Most libraries manage their tasks using an integrated library system (also known as an ILS, or ILMS, integrated library management system) that provides an automated package of library services. These library services are broken down into modules representing the range of tasks undertaken by library staff. The modules include:

- acquisitions (ordering, receiving, and invoicing resources)
- cataloging (classifying and indexing resources)
- serials (tracking holdings of journals)
- circulation (lending resources to patrons and receiving them back)
- the OPAC (library catalog display, the public interface for users).

In many integrated library management systems, Z39.50 standards are widely used for searching and retrieving information from other databases.

There are standard procedures for many of the day-to-day library tasks. In acquisitions sections, libraries record a standard set of details - author, title, edition, date of publication and so on - to identify the items they order. In the integrated library system, catalogers access these entries, and create catalog records adding further details to this basic information.

Items are then shelved using standard procedures, so that clients and library staff can locate them easily.

In addition to the standard rules and procedures, each library has its own preferred methods of performing some tasks. These methods arise from (among other things):

- the library's history – 'We've always done it like that.'
- the needs of clients – 'Our managing director insists on being first to see the new journals.'
- the peculiarities of the library's system – 'It seems to work faster if you scan the item's barcode first.'

Some standards used in libraries are international. At higher levels of library work, items are cataloged using the descriptive cataloging guidelines known as *Resource description and access (RDA)*, along with *MARC formats, Library of Congress* or *Dewey decimal classification* and *Library of Congress subject headings*.

Communication Skills

Being able to communicate effectively is a basic requirement of working in any information agency. Every aspect of the work - from identifying exactly what clients want, to locating and providing the information - requires good communication skills.

In particular, library staff need to be able to:

- make clients feel welcome and comfortable
- find out exactly what clients wish to know

- teach clients to find information for themselves
- work as a team with other staff members
- liaise with other information agencies
- consult with professional colleagues
- communicate information
- help clients to pursue other sources of information.

REVISION QUIZ 1.2

Use the following questions to revise your understanding of basic library skills. You do not need to write down the answers.

1. What skills are needed by someone working in a library?

   Technical + communication skills

2. What are the benefits of electronic resources?

   - info provided faster, at any time + more conveniently
   - they don't take up space, can't be stolen/destroyed, allow more than 1
     user to access info at a time

3. Give three examples of the following types of resources:
   a. Audio
   - audiobooks
   - mp3
   - vinyl records

   b. Electronic
   - DVD
   - video tapes
   - e-books

   c. Images
   - drawings
   - maps
   - prints

   d. Text
   - pamphlets
   - manuscripts
   - ephemera

CHAPTER TWO
Bibliographic Information

Introduction

Library collections—both large and small—are most valuable when resources can be easily located. Methods of organization include:

- arranging items on shelves according to their subject and/or author or title
- describing each item, including its title, author and subject(s), and providing these details in a library catalog
- listing items in a bibliography or subject guide
- contributing information about the collection to databases maintained outside the library (e.g., contributing your library holdings to union catalogs).

Keeping track of all the items in a collection, and recording them in such a way that they can be found when needed, is called **bibliographic control.** The methods of bibliographic control listed above require the creation of bibliographic information.

What Is Bibliographic Information?

Bibliographic information describes and represents the items in a collection. The information is designed to assist users to:

- find a resource that matches their search criteria
- identify the resource: from a list, confirm which one(s) they want and distinguish it from other resources with similar characteristics
- select a format that is appropriate to their needs
- obtain the resource.

The information for each resource is stored in a **bibliographic record**, which usually includes the following data elements:

- the title
- names associated with the resource such as a composer, author or illustrator
- a description of the format and size, such as how many pages are in a book
- other titles associated with the resource such as a series, if there is one
- the subject (what the resource is about) or a summary of the content
- where to find the item on a shelf in the library, or online.

The separate elements are commonly known as **bibliographic data** because the information is created and stored in a way that makes it easy for computer programs to work with it.

Here is an example of bibliographic data about a book.

	AUTHOR	Mein Smith, Philippa.
	TITLE	A concise history of New Zealand / by Philippa Mein Smith.
	PUBLISHER	Cambridge : Cambridge University Press, 2012.
	EDITION	2nd edition
	DESCRIPTION	xix, 348 pages : illustrations, maps ; 22 cm
	SERIES	Cambridge concise histories

LOCATION	CALL #	STATUS
6th floor	DU420. M45 2012	Available

Image Copyright © 2012 Philippa Mein Smith. Reprinted with the permission of Cambridge University Press.

The bibliographic record helps library users decide whether the item is the exact one they require or whether it contains the information they want.

 Here is an example of bibliographic data about an audio book.

	TITLE	The fault in our stars Written by John Green	
	PUBLISHED	Tullamarine, Victoria : Brilliance Audio, 2013	
	READ BY	Kate Rudd	
	FORMAT	6 CDs (7 hours 19 minutes)	
	SUMMARY	The story of Hazel and Augustus, two Indianapolis teenagers who meet at a Cancer Kid Support Group.	

CALL NO.	BARCODE	STATUS	LOCATION
T Green	191934	In	Main

The bibliographic data in this record includes a description of the format of the item, which helps library users decide whether they can to take it on holiday (in which case they would need a CD player).

Standardized Bibliographic Information

Bibliographic information that is created according to established instructions is considered to be standardized. Standardized bibliographic information makes it possible for libraries to share records that describe the resources in their collections. Libraries have standardized and shared their bibliographic data—especially catalog records—for many decades.

For example, if a library in Vancouver, Canada and a library in Brisbane, Australia have exactly the same book in their collections, it makes sense for them to share the bibliographic record created by (for example) the Library of Congress in the USA. Similarly, it is much easier for users of the records to deal with one standard format containing elements that are recognizable and reliable when they use different libraries.

Elements of Bibliographic Records

A bibliographic record consists of the following bits of data, also known as elements:

element name	element content
author	who is responsible for the intellectual or artistic content
title	what the resource is called
publication statement	where, by whom and when was it published
copyright date	when copyright was granted for the resource
edition	a particular form or version of a published resource, often numbered
format	the physical packaging of the content, such as a printed book
physical characteristics	the number and type of units, such as number of pages
standard number(s)	registered numbers such as ISBN
subject	what is the resource about

 Here is an example of a title page and verso (i.e., back) of the title page, which are the main places (but not the only places) to find bibliographic information about a book.

EYRIE

by Tim Winton

Farrar, Straus and Giroux

Farrar, Straus and Giroux, New York

First North American edition

copyright ©2013 by Tim Winton

all rights reserved

Originally published in 2013

by Hamish Hamilton,

an imprint of Penguin Books, Australia

Published in the United States

by Farrar, Straus and Giroux

First American Edition, 2014

ISBN 978-0374151348

The bibliographic data to describe this book is below. It contains a description of the book and the access points under which a library user might look for it.

element name	element content
author	Tim Winton
title	Eyrie
publication statement	New York: Farrar, Straus and Giroux, 2014
copyright date	© 2013
edition (if any)	First North American edition
format	printed book
physical characteristics	432 pages ; 24 cm
number(s)	ISBN 978-0374151348
subject	Interpersonal relations -- Fiction

The content of the bibliographic description is a combination of words taken from the item itself (such as the title) and words taken from controlled lists of terms that represent subjects. The words and phrases that are searchable by computer are referred to as **access points**. Access points are names and words indexed by the computer for quick retrieval of bibliographic descriptions.

For example, sometimes a library user wants to read a resource by a particular author. Authors' names and titles are access points (they are indexed and searchable) so it is easy to search by a name or title to determine whether a library owns works by a particular person. Some library users want to read a book on a topic and they do not mind who wrote it. The access point most useful to them is the **subject** (also known as subject heading) which provides searchable words that make it easy to find only the items in a collection about a particular topic.

EXERCISE 2.1

Below are title pages and versos for books. Note in the template provided the information you think may help a library patron to identify the work.

1.

THE OIL MAN AND THE SEA
~ ARNO KOPECKY ~

Navigating the Northern Gateway

Douglas & McIntyre

Copyright ©2013 Arno Kopecky
Photographs copyright © Ilja Herb except where noted

All rights reserved.
Douglas & McIntyre (2013) Ltd.
P.O. Box 219, Madeira Park, BC VON 2H0

ISBN: 978-1-77100-107-6(paper)   ISBN: 978-77100-108-3(ebook)

Edited by Trena White
Copy edit by Elaine Park, Indexed by Morgan Davies
Cover and interior design by Jessica Sullivan
Cover spot illustrations by Michael Nicoll Yahgulanaas
Map by Roger Handling

Printed in Canada

The book has 264 pages, a map, color and black & white photographs, an index.

Title	
Author, editors, compilers, translators, illustrators, etc.	
Place(s) of publication	
Name of publisher(s)	
Copyright date	
Edition, if any	
Physical characteristics	
Series (if any)	
Notes – any other information that could help to find or verify the item	
Standard number(s)	

2.

Newmarket Shooting Script Series

SNOW FALLING ON CEDARS

Screenplay by
Ron Bass and Scott Hicks

Based on the novel by
David Guterson
Commentaries by
Scott Hicks and Kathleen Kennedy

NEWMARKET PRESS – NEW YORK

Design and compilation copyright © 1999 by Newmarket Press. All rights reserved.

This book is published simultaneously
in the United States of America and in Canada.

First Edition
ISBN 1-55704-372-8 (pb)

The book has 166 pages with illustrations. It is 24 cm high.

Title	
Author, editors, compilers, translators, illustrators, etc.	
Place(s) of publication	
Name of publisher(s)	
Copyright date	
Edition, if any	
Physical characteristics	
Series (if any)	
Notes – any other information that could help to find or verify the item	
Standard number(s)	

Standards for Bibliographic Data

Catalog records form the basis of bibliographic control in most libraries. For many decades these catalog records were created using the International Standard Bibliographic Description (ISBD) developed by the International Federation of Library Associations and Institutions (IFLA). This is the standard used in the *Anglo-American cataloguing rules second edition (AACR2)*. There are millions of catalog records in hundreds of catalogs around the world that were created using AACR2.

AACR2 was developed with card catalogs in mind. These rules instructed catalogers to abbreviate or omit some information so that the description would fit on catalog cards, which were filed alphabetically in drawers. Although space is not limited in the online environment, AACR2 continued to be used long after online catalogs were implemented.

In 2013 the national libraries of Australia, Canada, Germany, USA and other countries adopted a new set of guidelines for cataloging library collections called *RDA: Resource Description and Access*. Bibliographic data created with RDA is created with computer algorithms and search engines in mind. Information is mostly transcribed into the record as it appears on the item, without omissions or abbreviations introduced by the cataloger.

Many libraries implemented RDA as of 2013 or later; some continue to use AACR2. As a result, library catalogs often contain bibliographic descriptions based on both AACR2 and RDA, depending on when the catalog record was created. It is therefore important to be aware of the basic features of both ISBD (that was the basis for AACR2 rules) and RDA.

International Standard Bibliographic Description (ISBD)

This standard provided a framework for creating bibliographic descriptions in a consistent, human-readable form. It formed the basis of AACR2 cataloging. Following ISBD allowed libraries to exchange catalog records with other libraries around the world. Although the new RDA guidelines are based on a different framework, some of ISBD's descriptive elements, and its punctuation, are incorporated into RDA-compliant cataloging.

The ISBD:
- lists all elements required to describe and identify all types of material
- assigns an order to the elements
- prescribes punctuation to precede each element.

ISBD defines nine areas of description:

    Area 0: Content form and media type
    Area 1: Title and statement of responsibility
    Area 2: Edition
    Area 3: Material or type of resource
    Area 4: Publication, production, distribution, etc.,
    Area 5: Material description
    Area 6: Series and multipart monographic resource
    Area 7: Notes
    Area 8: Resource identifier and terms of availability

Area 0 was recently added to the ISBD areas of description, to make it more compatible with the new RDA standard. Area 0 contains terminology to describe various formats of resources, performing the same role as RDA's 'content type', 'media type' and 'carrier type' elements. Some examples of Area 0 terminology are:

Area 0 Terms	Format
Image (cartographic ; tactile)	a map meant to be touched
Music (performed) : audio	an audio CD
Music (notated)	a sheet of music
Spoken word : audio	an audio book
Text: unmediated	a printed book
Text : electronic	an electronic book or website

In AACR2 cataloging, some resources require all areas of description, some do not. For example, if there is no edition statement on a particular resource, that area is omitted.

The areas may be reorganized in a library catalog display (OPAC), and given user-friendly labels or graphics so as to omit terms the general public does not use. For example, Area 0 might be displayed as an icon depicting the physical format, or as text.

    Here is an example catalog display:

KATE L. TURABIAN **A Manual for Writers** OF RESEARCH PAPERS, THESES, AND DISSERTATIONS *Chicago Style for Students & Researchers* **Eighth Edition** REVISED BY WAYNE C. BOOTH, GREGORY G. COLOMB, JOSEPH W. WILLIAMS, AND THE UNIVERSITY OF CHICAGO PRESS EDITORIAL STAFF Copyright © 2013 Kate L. Turabian. Reprinted with the permission of University of Chicago Press.	**AUTHOR**	Turabian, Kate L.
	TITLE	A manual for writers of research papers, theses, and dissertations : Chicago style for students and researchers / Kate L. Turabian ; revised by Wayne C. Booth, Gregory G. Colomb, Joseph M. Williams, and University of Chicago Press editorial staff
	PUBLISHED	Chicago : University of Chicago Press, 2013
	EDITION	Eighth edition
	DESCRIPTION	xv, 448 pages : illustrations ; 23 cm
	SERIES	Chicago guides to writing, editing, and publishing
	NOTES	Includes bibliographical references (pages 409-433) and index
	ISBN	9780226816388
	LOCATION	808.0662 TUR

Here is the underlying bibliographic data in ISBD order:

Area 0	Text : unmediated
Area 1	A manual for writers of research papers, theses, and dissertations : Chicago style for students and researchers / Kate L. Turabian ; revised by Wayne C. Booth, Gregory G. Colomb, Joseph M. Williams, and University of Chicago Press editorial staff
Area 2	Eighth edition
Area 3	
Area 4	Chicago : University of Chicago Press, 2013
Area 5	xv, 448 pages : illustrations ; 23 cm
Area 6	(Chicago guides to writing, editing, and publishing)
Area 7	Includes bibliographical references (pages 409-433) and index
Area 8	ISBN 9780226816388 (pbk.) : USD18.00

Punctuation Marks

Standardized punctuation is used to separate the data elements within each ISBD area of description. For example, an equals sign is used between parallel titles (titles in different languages); a diagonal slash is used between the title and author statements.

Standardized punctuation makes it easier to interpret bibliographic records in any library catalog anywhere around the world, even when one does not understand the language of the description.

Since punctuation acts to indicate different areas, it has played an important role in bibliographic descriptions and displays, and continues to do so. The new RDA standard includes ISBD punctuation as an appendix, for those libraries that wish to use it when coding bibliographic data.

Common punctuation marks used in ISBD:

, comma	: colon	-- dash
/ diagonal slash	= equals sign	. full stop/period
- hyphen	( ) parentheses	+ plus sign
; semicolon	[ ] square brackets	

 EXERCISE 2.2

Answer the following questions about ISBD punctuation.

1. In the example above, *A manual for writers of research papers, theses, and dissertations*:

a. what punctuation mark separates the title from the author statement?

b. what punctuation mark is used between each element in the publication statement?

2. Which of the following use correct ISBD punctuation? (*More than one of these is correct.*)

   a. The Oxford companion to music, by Percy A. Scholes.

   b. xliii, 1189 pages, 185 pages of plates : illustrations ; 24 cm.

   c. The Oxford companion to music / by Percy A. Scholes.

   d. The Oxford companion to music : by Percy A. Scholes.

   e. xliii, 1189 pages; 185 pages of plates. Illustrations, 24 cm.

3. Add ISBD punctuation to the following:

   a. Morocco modern   Herbert Ypma

   b. New York   Thames & Hudson   2010

   c. 157 pages   color illustrations   22 cm

   d. The red and the blacklist   the intimate memoir of a Hollywood expatriate   Norma Barzman

   e. New York   Thunder's Mouth Press   2003

   f. xi   464 pages   8 unnumbered pages of plates   portraits   24 cm

Resource Description and Access (RDA)

This standard is designed for the digital world and represents a change in direction for cataloging. It uses IFLA's *Functional Requirements for Bibliographic Records* (FRBR) as its framework rather than ISBD. The FRBR framework underlies the cataloging guidelines used in RDA. FRBR focuses on the user tasks of finding, identifying, selecting and obtaining material, and recommends the basic bibliographic information needed in a catalog record.

RDA provides the cataloger with instructions and guidelines for recording bibliographic data. RDA uses key bibliographic elements of interest to users (e.g., title, statement of responsibility, physical details) and emphasizes their relationships. It deals with *what* to record, not *how* to record it.

RDA is described as a 'content standard'. This means it provides instructions on recording the *content* of resources, not on how the information can be displayed or encoded. Because RDA is a 'format neutral' content standard—not tied to any particular encoding scheme—it can be used by a range of cultural collecting agencies like museums and archives, as well as libraries. This provides both flexibility and greater interoperability for the exchange of catalog records.

You may notice some differences between AACR2 and RDA bibliographic records, but the elements included and the ways in which they are displayed in library catalogs are very similar. This introduction will give you a foundation for understanding catalog displays. Full cataloging procedures are not dealt with in this book since they are quite complex and need to be studied separately. Cataloging procedures are explained in detail in *Learn cataloging the RDA way* by Lynn Farkas and Helen Rowe.

 Here is a resource cataloged using RDA and AACR2. The differences between them are highlighted in bold in the RDA record, and explained below. Note the additional information provided in the RDA record, and the efforts made to use 'plain English' terms rather than abbreviations.

RDA		**AACR2**	
CREATOR	McCall Smith, Alexander, 1948- **,author.**	AUTHOR	McCall Smith, Alexander, 1948- .
TITLE	The importance of being seven : a 44 Scotland Street novel / Alexander McCall Smith; illustrations by Iain McIntosh.	TITLE	The importance of being seven : a 44 Scotland Street novel / Alexander McCall Smith.
PUBLISHED	New York : Anchor Books, 2012.	PUBLISHED	New York : Anchor Books, 2012, c2010.
COPYRIGHT	©2010.		
EDITION	**First Anchor Books edition.**	EDITION	1ˢᵗ Anchor Books ed.
DESCRIPTION	311 **pages: illustrations**; 22 cm.	DESCRIPTION	311 p.: ill.; 22 cm.
CONTENT	**text**		
MEDIA	**unmediated**		
CARRIER	**volume**		

1. **Creator field** – RDA includes more information about what type of relationship the person has to the resource – he is the author (as opposed to editor, composer, etc.).
2. **Copyright field** – Copyright statements are given more prominence in RDA.
3. **Edition field** – RDA transcribes information as it appears on the resource and doesn't use abbreviations for the sake of convention.
4. **Description field** – RDA avoids abbreviations for 'pages' and 'illustrations' (unlike AACR2 which has a great many abbreviations).
5. **Content, Media, Carrier fields** – these are RDA elements which indicate what type of item the resource is (text); what type of media is needed to view it (none, it is unmediated); and how it is packaged (in a physical volume). These elements are similar to ISBD Area 0 'Content form and media type'.

EXERCISE 2.3

Read the catalog displays below and answer the questions about each.

1.

Saved by cake	
AUTHOR:	Marian Keyes ; photography by Alistair Richardson.
PUBLISHER:	London : Michael Joseph, 2012.
SUMMARY:	During her struggles with depression, Marian Keyes discovered that baking helped her cope. Included in this book are her simple recipes for cakes, cupcakes and cookies.
DESCRIPTION:	230 pages : color illustrations ; 24 cm.
CONTENT:	text
MEDIA:	unmediated
CARRIER:	volume
CONTENTS:	Introduction -- Equipment list -- Some rules -- Techniques and helpful hints -- Classics -- Cupcakes -- Cheesecakes -- Liquid cakes -- Pastry -- Meringues and macaroons -- Biscuits and cookies -- Fruit and veg -- Chocolate.
NOTES:	Includes index.
SUBJECTS:	Keyes, Marian -- Mental health.
	Cake.
	Depression, Mental -- Popular works.
ISBN:	9780718158897 071815889X
OCLC:	759584428

a.   By what name(s) is this work known that might be searched by a library patron?

b.   What format is it? How can you tell?

c.   What names are associated with this work? What are the role(s) of people named?

d.   What is the work about? How can you tell?

e.   What numbers are associated with this work?

2.

TITLE:	Soccer unites the world / National Geographic Maps.
AUTHOR:	National Geographic Maps (Firm);
	National Geographic Society (U.S.)
IMPRINT:	Washington, D.C. : National Geographic Society, 2006.
COPYRIGHT:	©2006.
DESCRIPTION:	1 map : color ; 31 x 46 cm., on sheet 52 x 61 cm., folded to 13 x 16 cm.
SCALE:	1:78,630,000. 1 in. = 1,241 miles ; Winkel Tripel projection
CONTENT:	cartographic image
MEDIA:	unmediated
CARRIER:	sheet
NOTES:	Panel title.
	"Supplement to National Geographic, June 2006."
	"Printed April 2006."
	Opposite side has: The Beautiful Game.
SUMMARY:	Includes pie charts showing percentages of participation in soccer by populations of North America, South America, Europe, Asia, and Africa, information on economics of soccer in comparison with other team sports, a timeline of historical development of the modern game, diagrams of characteristic plays by teams from Brazil, Germany, Italy, and England, text and illustrations of dribbling moves, an illustration of construction of a soccer ball, brief biographies of 4 prominent soccer players.
SUBJECTS:	Soccer -- Maps.
OTHER TITLES:	Beautiful game

a. By what name(s) is this work known that might be searched by a library patron?

b. What format is it? How can you tell?

c. What is the scale and projection method?

d. What names are associated with this work?

3.

TITLE:	Chansons d'amour Edith Piaf
CREATOR:	Edith Piaf, singer.
IMPRINT:	London : ELAP, 2001.
COPYRIGHT:	Ⓟ2001.
DESCRIPTION:	1 sound disc (CD) : digital, mono. ; 12 cm.
CONTENT:	performed music
MEDIA:	audio
CARRIER:	audio disc
CONTENTS:	Le petit homme – Un refrain courait dans la rue – C'est pour ça – Dans les prisons de Nantes – Céline – Le chant du pirate – Adieu mon coeur – Regarde–moi toujours comme ça – Coup de grisou – Un monsieur me suit dans la rue – Tu es partout – Le brun et le blond – Simple comme bonjour – Jimmy, c'est lui – La Julie jolie – La java de Cézique.
SUBJECTS:	Popular music.
	Songs, French.

a. By what name(s) is this work known that might be searched by a library patron?

b. What format is it? How can you tell?

c. What is the role of Edith Piaf?

d. What information is given in the contents field?

Classification Numbers

Classification refers to the organization of library materials by subject. Each resource in a collection is assigned a classification number which indicates the subject of the resource. There are two major classification schemes:

- Dewey Decimal Classification (DDC)
- Library of Congress Classification (LCC).

There are also several specialized classification schemes that suit particular types of information (such as medical information) or special types of libraries (such as corporate libraries). Classification is treated in greater detail in Chapter 9 of this workbook that discusses the shelving of physical resources.

Call Numbers

Each physical item in a collection is assigned a unique call number which acts as an 'address' to help shelvers maintain the stacks in proper order and allow users to find the exact item they want on the shelf. Call numbers are constructed by combining a classification number with a book number. A book number is notation (letters and numbers) based on the author or the title of the item, and may include the date of publication.

Dewey Decimal Classification (DDC)

Dewey Decimal Classification organizes all knowledge into 10 broad disciplines and uses numbers to represent subjects.

Dewey call numbers include the classification number and the book number.

 Here is an example of a DDC call number.
636.7   *DDC number for the subject Dogs*
HEW   *book number (first 3 letters of the author's last name Heward)*

Library of Congress Classification (LCC)

Library of Congress Classification organizes all knowledge into 21 broad disciplines and uses a combination of letters and numbers to represent subjects.

LCC call numbers include the classification number, a book number (also called a Cutter number) and the date of publication.

 Here is an example of an LC call number.
GV1787   *LCC number for the subject Ballet*
.S37 2005   *book number (notation for the title) and date of publication*

Location Symbols

The location symbol indicates where the item is housed, identifying a particular area or room in the library or building. For example, a reference work may have 'R' or 'REF'; an audiovisual item may have 'AV' as their location symbols. Location symbols may also indicate a branch of a library system that has more than one location. They are often used in combination with a call number to give additional information about where an item can be found.

 Here are examples of call numbers with location symbols.

REF	CITY	AV	MAIN
636.7	362.4	GV1787	PR2877
HEW	THA	.S37	.B4
		2005	2010

CHAPTER THREE
The Catalog

Introduction

In the majority of libraries the most efficient way to find resources held in the collection is via the online catalog, usually referred to as the OPAC (**O**nline **P**ublic **A**ccess **C**atalog). The OPAC allows you to search and retrieve bibliographic data about the resources. The OPAC will tell you where resources are housed and whether physical resources are currently in the library or out on loan.

Searching the Catalog

Why is it more useful to search a catalog instead of browsing the shelves of the library to find a resource?

- Resources that contain information on a particular topic may be shelved in several different areas of the library, in special collections, in different formats or even in different branches of the library.
- The catalog provides details on the current status and availability of a resource (e.g., whether it is out on loan or whether it is being repaired).
- Items on order are usually listed in the catalog so a patron can see whether a new resource on their topic is about to arrive in the library.
- You would miss out on knowing what electronic resources are available on the topic if you only browse the shelves.

Access Points

The words that are indexed in bibliographic descriptions and can be searched in a library catalog are known as the **access points**. An access point is any part of the catalog record which enables a user to find the resource.

With online catalogs it is possible to have many access points. In theory, every element in a record is searchable, depending on the library catalog software. This means there is the potential to have more access points than was possible with a manual catalog. Most commonly, the access points for a resource would include:

- titles
- variations of the title that the resource may be known as
- authors
- additional people or organizations associated with the resource (editors, illustrators, etc.)
- series titles
- subjects

EXERCISE 3.1

Highlight all the access points you might expect in these catalog records.

1.

CALL NO	523.2 L253
AUTHOR	Lang, Kenneth R.
TITLE	The Cambridge guide to the solar system / Kenneth R. Lang.
EDITION	2nd edition
PUBLISHER	Cambridge : Cambridge University Press, 2011.
DESCRIPT'N	xxv, 475 pages : illustrations (some color) ; 29 cm.
ISBN	1) 0521198577 (hardback)
	2) 9780521198578 (hardback)
NOTE(S)	1) Includes bibliographical references and index.
SUBJECT	1) Solar system.
	2) Astronomy.

2.

TITLE:	2014 FIFA World Cup Brazil.
ALSO TITLED:	FIFA World Cup Brazil
	Brazil
CONTENT TYPE:	two-dimensional moving image.
CARRIER TYPE:	computer disc.
EDITION:	Xbox 360.
PUBLISHED:	Geneva, Switzerland Electronic Arts, [c2014]
DESCRIPTION:	1 computer disc : DVD video, sound, colour ; 4 3/4 in.
STANDARD NUMBER:	5030944112403
TECHNICAL DETAILS:	System requirements: Xbox 360; 20 MB to save game ; HDTV 720p/1080i/1080p; in-game Dolby digital.
SUMMARY:	Lead your country to FIFA World Cup glory while experiencing all the fun, excitement and drama of soccer's greatest event.
NOTES:	Title from disc label.
	1-4 players ; 2 online multiplayer.
	Censorship classification : G.
	Game in English and Spanish.
SUBJECTS:	World Cup (Soccer) (2014 : Brazil)

Authority Control

Authority control is the maintenance of standard forms of access points found in the catalog. This enables library users to locate information using consistent subject and name headings.

For example, Eric Arthur Blair did not write under his own name but used the name George Orwell when writing. To find anything that he wrote we would need to search the catalog under the name 'Orwell' not under 'Blair'.

Catalogers record decisions about the standard forms of access points, as well as the research that they have done to make those decisions, in an authority file. This file can be shared by the staff of one cataloging department or by a consortium of libraries or even internationally via the Internet so that other catalogers do not have to re-create headings or research them again. References made to and from the headings are also recorded in this file.

 Using the example of George Orwell, and searching an authority file, such as the Libraries Australia Authority File, we find the following authority record:

AUTHORITY TYPE:	Name.
HEADING:	Orwell, George, 1903-1950
USED FOR:	Orwell, George
	Aūrūal, Jūrj
	Blair, Eric Arthur, 1903-1950

Searching for either 'Blair, Eric Arthur' or 'Orwell, George' directs you to this authority record which includes any other names that Orwell has used or is known by. Looking at this authority record you'll see there is also a Used For note for 'Aūrūal, Jūrj'. If someone searched 'Aūrūal, Jūrj' in this authority file they would be directed to 'Orwell, George' (which is the authorized access point).

Authority control is an important part of bibliographic control because it provides controlled vocabulary that gives consistent information about a resource and enables that resource to be linked to other resources. As keyword searching is a powerful technology for searching full text databases, maintaining consistency with access points ensures links will continue to be made between resources.

Authority Records

An authority record indicates the chosen access point for a person, family, place, corporate body, series or title. It provides information about the preferred and non-preferred terms (called authorized access points and variant access points), as well as notes about how these were derived. There are four types of authority records:
- Name
- Subject
- Series
- Preferred Title of the Work/Expression (previously known as Uniform Title).

Name Authority Records

Establishing name authority records involves the use of cataloging guidelines, such as RDA, to decide on the correct form of the access point and whether a date or affiliation should be included. Catalogers might also use reference sources such as *Who's who, Chambers biographical dictionary, Merriam-Webster's biographical dictionary, Monash biographical dictionary of 20th century Australia* and so on to find dates of birth and death, or the full form of names.

Subject Authority Records

Most libraries establish their subject headings using *Library of Congress subject headings,* http://id.loc.gov/authorities/subjects.html. School libraries in Australia and New Zealand use the *SCIS subject headings list,* produced by the Schools Catalog Information Service (SCIS), http://www2.curriculum.edu.au/subject_heading_lists.html, while school libraries in North America use *Sears list of subject headings,* published by H. W. Wilson http://www.hwwilsoninprint.com/sears.php. Medical libraries often use *Medical subject headings (MeSH),* http://www.nlm.nih.gov/mesh/MBrowser.html, created by the United States National Library of Medicine. Other libraries may use their own subject thesaurus to create their subject headings.

Authority Files

We have already discussed authority records. How do these differ from authority files? An authority file is a collection of authority records containing the authorized access points for names, series and subjects. Name authority files generally include preferred titles of works/expressions and series in addition to personal and corporate names.

Libraries might maintain their own local authority file, or use authority files available online to find and verify access points for their catalog. Remember, access points include names, series and subjects.

Authority control is incorporated into many library management systems. Authority files are created using the cataloging guidelines in *Resource description and access (RDA)*.

The largest authority file for names is the *Library of Congress authorities*. Libraries can purchase access to the online version of this from vendors. This authority file is also available free of charge on the Library of Congress Linked Data Service website http://id.loc.gov/, and on the Library of Congress Authorities website http://authorities.loc.gov.

The major authority file for subjects is the *Library of Congress subject headings (LCSH)*. This file has been available in print as a multivolume set, however the 35th edition published in 2013 was the last edition to be printed. LCSH continues to be updated and is available as free downloadable pdf files. The latest edition, the 36th edition, selected in June 2014, is available free of charge at http://www.loc.gov/aba/cataloging/subject/, and includes documentation on how to apply the subject headings. LCSH is also accessible online as part of the subscription to Classification Web from the Library of Congress at http://classificationweb.net/.

Access to *Canadian subject headings (CSH)* and names maintained by the Library and Archives of Canada are available online, free of charge, at http://www.bac-lac.gc.ca/eng/services/canadian-subject-headings/Pages/canadian-subject-headings.aspx.

Australian names and subject headings are listed in the Australian National Bibliographic Database (ANBD) on Libraries Australia at http://www.nla.gov.au/librariesaustralia/services/cataloging/standards/lcsh-extension/. These headings are particularly useful for Australian libraries, since not all Australian headings are included in the Library of Congress lists.

Large cataloging networks such as OCLC also maintain their own authority files.

References

A reference is a direction or signpost in the catalog from one access point to another, so that library users can find all related entries. Libraries use three types of references:

- variant access points ('see' references)
- authorized access points for related entities ('see also' references)
- explanatory references.

Variant Access Points

A **variant access point** is a non-preferred variation of a title or name. It directs the user from an access point which is not used to an authorized access point, which is used. The unused (or non-preferred) forms may result from:

- change of name - when people change their name, their previous name is no longer used
- confusion about which part of a name to use—e.g., a searcher may not know whether to look for Jean de la Fontaine (a French writer) under 'de', 'la' or 'Fontaine'
- different information available to catalogers at different times
- a different form of name preferred by the person.

Variant access points were traditionally called 'see references' in catalogs and indexing services.

These signposts are incorporated into library systems in a variety of ways. Here is an example:

AUTHORITY TYPE:	Name.
LC NUMBER:	n 50037217
HEADING:	Franklin, Miles, 1879-1954
USED FOR:	Franklin, Stella Maria Sarah Miles, 1879-1954
	Franklin, Stella Miles, 1879-1954
	Franklin, Stella, 1879-1954
	Franklin, Stella Maria Miles Lampe, 1879-1954

In this instance, the searcher looked for 'Franklin, Stella Maria Miles Lampe' in the authority file. They were automatically directed to the authority record for the authorized access point, 'Franklin, Miles', and were not required to conduct another search to find the correct form of the name in the catalog.

This authority record shows that the author did not use her full name on her works, but wrote them under the name 'Miles Franklin'.

Authorized Access Points for a Related Entity

An **authorized access point for a related entity** directs the catalog user to a related entry or name. It provides a direction from one authorized access point to another when both are used in the catalog. It is normally used when a person or corporate body is entered under two or more different names. This happens most often when corporate bodies change their names. Authorized access points for related entities were traditionally called 'see also references' in catalogs and indexing services.

AUTHORITY TYPE:	Name.
HEADING:	United Nations Library (Geneva, Switzerland)
USED FOR:	United Nations. European Office, Library
	United Nations. United Nations Library (Geneva, Switzerland)
	Geneva (Switzerland). Library of the United Nations
	United Nations. European Office. United Nations Library
SEE ALSO:	League of Nations Library

AUTHORITY TYPE:	Name.
HEADING:	League of Nations Library
USED FOR:	League of Nations Library
	League of Nations. Secretariat. League of Nations Library
	League of Nations. Secretariat. Library
	Geneva (Switzerland). League of Nations Library

These authority records show that the 'League of Nations Library' and the 'United Nations Library (Geneva, Switzerland)' are both authorized access points for this corporate body. The authority file contains an authority record for each of the corporate bodies, because they were both the official name of the library at different times in the library's history. Resources are cataloged according to the name of the authorized access point at the time the resource was published. Therefore, it would be possible, and correct, for a catalog to contain both of these access points in its authority file.

Explanatory References

An explanatory reference provides more detailed guidance than is given for variant access points and authorized access points for related entities, by providing notes which explain the history of an organization. For example:

AUTHORITY TYPE:	Name.
HEADING:	League of Red Cross Societies
USED FOR:	Ligue des sociétiés de la Croix-Rouge
	Liga drusltava Crvenog krsta
SEE ALSO:	bnnn League of Red Cross and Red Crescent Societies
NOTES:	In 1983 the League of Red Cross Societies changed its name to League of Red Cross and Red Crescent Societies.

AUTHORITY TYPE:	Name.
HEADING:	League of Red Cross and Red Crescent Societies
USED FOR:	Liga de Sociedades de la Cruz Roja y de la Media Luna Roja
SEE ALSO:	bnnn International Federation of Red Cross and Red Crescent Societies
NOTES:	In 1983 the League of Red Cross Societies changed its name to League of Red Cross and Red Crescent Societies. In November 1991 the League of Red Cross and Red Crescent Societies changed its name to International Federation of Red Cross and Red Crescent Societies.

AUTHORITY TYPE:	Name.
HEADING:	International Federation of Red Cross and Red Crescent Societies
NOTES:	In November 1991 the League of Red Cross and Red Crescent Societies changed its name to International Federation of Red Cross and Red Crescent Societies.

Many explanatory references are to be found in major authority files. Others are created by individual libraries to explain particular cataloging usage and practices.

 Here are some further examples of authority records with explanatory references:

AUTHORITY TYPE:	Name.
HEADING:	Australia British Empire Games Association
NOTES:	Ca. 1952 the Australian British Empire Games Association changed its name to the Australian British Empire and Commonwealth Games Association. In 1966 the name was changed to the Australian British Commonwealth Games Association, and in 1974 it became the Australian Commonwealth Games Association. Works by these bodies are found under the name used at the time of publication.

AUTHORITY TYPE:	Name.
HEADING:	Australian British Empire and Commonwealth Games Association
SEE ALSO:	annn Australian British Empire Games Association
	bnnn Australian Commonwealth Games Association
NOTES:	Ca. 1952 the Australian British Empire Games Association changed its name to the Australian British Empire and Commonwealth Games Association. In 1966 the name was changed to the Australian British Commonwealth Games Association, and in 1974 it became the Australian Commonwealth Games Association. Works by these bodies are found under the name used at the time of publication.

AUTHORITY TYPE:	Name.
HEADING:	Australian British Commonwealth Games Association
SEE ALSO:	bnnn Australian Commonwealth Games Association
	annn Australian British Empire and Commonwealth Games Association
	annn Australian British Empire Games Association
NOTES:	Ca. 1952 the Australian British Empire Games Association changed its name to the Australian British Empire and Commonwealth Games Association. In 1966 the name was changed to the Australian British Commonwealth Games Association, and in 1974 it became the Australian Commonwealth Games Association. Works by these bodies are found under the name used at the time of publication.

AUTHORITY TYPE:	Name.
HEADING:	Australian Commonwealth Games Association
SEE ALSO:	annn Australian British Empire Games Association
NOTES:	Ca. 1952 the Australian British Empire Games Association changed its name to the Australian British Empire and Commonwealth Games Association. In 1966 the name was changed to the Australian British Commonwealth Games Association, and in 1974 it became the Australian Commonwealth Games Association. Works by these bodies are found under the name used at the time of publication.

The explanatory reference above shows the history of the name changes of this organization. Publications are cataloged using the name of the organization that was current at the time of publication. Therefore, it would be possible for a library catalog to have all of these access points in its authority file.

AUTHORITY TYPE:	Name.
LC NUMBER:	n 50001506 no 98025183
HEADING:	Armstrong, Louis, 1901-1971
BIRTH:	19010804
	New Orleans, La.
DEATH:	19710706
	New York, N.Y.
FIELDS OF ACTIVITY	jazz
USED FOR:	Armstrong, Satchmo, 1901-1971
	Satchmo, 1901-1971

This set of records gives **Armstrong, Louis, 1900-1971** as the correct authorized access point. Each of the 'Used for' references identifies a non-preferred access point, so catalogers should use them as variant access points.

EXERCISE 3.2

Look carefully at the catalog displays below, and answer the following questions.

1.

AUTHORITY TYPE:	Name.
HEADING:	Menzies, Robert, Sir, 1894-1978
USED FOR:	Menzies, Robert, 1894-1978
	Menzies, R. G. (Robert Gordon), Sir, 1894-1978
	Menzies, Robert Gordon, Sir, 1894-1978
SEE ALSO:	Australia. Prime Minister

a. Which is the authorized access point?

b. Does this library use the access point 'Menzies, R. G. (Robert Gordon), Sir, 1894-1978' for any works by this author?

2.

AUTHORITY TYPE:	Name.
HEADING:	International Federation of Library Associations
USED FOR:	I.F.L.A.
SEE ALSO:	International Federation of Library Associations and Institutions
NOTES:	The name of the International Federation of Library Associations was expanded to International Federation of Library Associations and Institutions with the adoption of a new constitution in August, 1976.

    a. Is the access point 'International Federation of Library Associations' used in this catalog?

    b. Is the access point 'International Federation of Library Associations and Institutions' also used?

EXERCISE 3.3

Look carefully at the records below, and answer the following questions.

1.

AUTHORITY TYPE:	Name.
HEADING:	Rowling, J. K.
USED FOR:	Rowling, Joanne K, (Joanne Kathleen)
	Rowling, Jo
	Rowlingová, Joanne K.
SEE ALSO:	Galbraith, Robert
NOTES:	Harry Potter, 1998 CIP title page (J. K. Rowling)
	The Washington post, 10-20-99 page C1 (J. K. Rowling, Joanne Kathleen Rowling, 34, creator of Harry Potter)
	J. K. Rowling, c2002: page 9 (Joanne Kathleen Rowling; Jo is still the name she likes to be called)

AUTHORITY TYPE:	Name.
DESCRIPTION CONVENTIONS:	rda
HEADING:	Galbraith, Robert
FIELDS OF ACTIVITY:	Crime fiction
	Detective and mystery stories
OCCUPATIONS:	Authors
USED FOR:	Galbraith, Robert, 1968-
SEE ALSO:	Rowling, J. K.
	Works by this author are identified by the name used in the item. For a listing of other names used by this author, search also under: Rowling, J. K.
NOTES:	The cuckoo's calling, 2013 title page (Robert Galbraith)
	Telegraph, viewed July 15, 2013 (J. K. Rowling unmasked as author of acclaimed detective novel. Writing under the pseudonym Robert Galbraith, the Harry Potter creator wrote a 450 page crime novel called The Cuckoo's Calling. The book is billed as a 'classic crime novel', written in the style of PD James and Ruth Rendell, according to the Sunday Times)

a. Which are the authorized access points to be used for this person in the catalog?

b. What will happen if a client looks up 'Rowling, Jo'?

c. Do all these entries refer to the same person?

2.

AUTHORITY TYPE:	Name.
HEADING:	Canada. Atmospheric Environment Service
USED FOR:	Canada. Dept. of the Environment. Atmospheric Environment Service
	Canada. Dept. of the Environment. Environnement atmosphérique
	Canada. Service de l'environnement atmosphérique
	Canada. Dept. of the Environment. Service de l'environnement atmosphérique
	Canada. Environnement atmosphérique
SEE ALSO:	Canada. Meteorological Branch
NOTES:	The Meterological Office of Canada was established in 1871. In 1877 the name was changed to Meteorological Service; in 1937, to Meteorological Division; in 1955, to Meteorological Branch; in April 1971, to Meteorological Service; and in June 1971, to Atmospheric Environment Service. Works are found under the name used at the time of publication.

a. Which is the authorized access point to be used for this organization in the catalog?

b. What does the 'see also' reference mean?

c. Might a catalog contain more than one of these access points? Under what circumstances?

MARC

Humans can easily read and interpret the text of bibliographic descriptions. In order to make the descriptions computer-friendly, it is necessary to 'markup' bibliographic data so that computers can read and work with it. **Markup** means adding punctuation such as angle brackets < > or notation such as numbers or letters to indicate what the data is.

There are various markup schemes, depending on where the data will be used and displayed.

Here are examples of ways to tell a computer that a piece of information is a title:

for web documents:	HTML	<title>Learn basic library skills</title>
for bibliographic data:	Dublin Core	<dc.title>Learn basic library skills</dc.title>
for bibliographic data:	MARC	245 $aLearn basic library skills.

The markup system used by libraries is MARC. MARC stands for **MA**chine **R**eadable **Catalog**ing. The MARC format is an international standard. MARC coding provides a way for computers to interpret the information found in a catalog record by labeling each piece of bibliographic information, so that automated systems can read and manipulate it.

MARC was developed to allow libraries to share cataloging by providing a format that can be read and understood by different library information systems. Today there are millions of MARC records available, with more being created daily by catalogers all over the world.

MARC bibliographic records consist of bibliographic descriptions of library materials, including books, serials, electronic resources, maps and so on.

MARC authority records consist of established access points, variant access points and, sometimes, notes that indicate the scope of an access point and the tools consulted to establish the access point.

Fields

In all databases, a record is a collection of related fields. The fields in a record in a MARC database contain the bibliographic information that forms the bibliographic record. These include the resource's physical description, the access points, the subject headings and the classification numbers.

The MARC record also contains fields that provide information required by the computer. These fields will not be discussed here. (For more details about the MARC record, see Chapter Six of *Learn cataloging the RDA way* by Lynn Farkas and Helen Rowe.)

Tags

Each field has an identifying label. This label is called a tag and consists of three characters. For example, the 'Title and Statement of Responsibility' field uses the tag '245'.

Indicators

Two additional characters, called indicators, are used in some fields to provide the computer with extra information.

 300 __ $a2 sound discs (mp3 + m4b) (19 hr. 52 min.) :$bdigital, stereo ;$c4 3/4 in.

In this field the indicators are not needed and are left blank.

 245 14 $aThe Viking dig :$bexcavations at York /$cRichard Hall.

The first indicator '1' instructs the computer to make an added entry for the title.
The second indicator '4' shows that four characters need to be ignored when the title is filed.

Subfields and Subfield Codes

The elements within a field are called subfields. Each subfield is introduced by a subfield code which is preceded by a subfield delimiter. (In this book we have used a dollar sign '$' as the delimiter. In other places the delimiter might be identified using a pipe symbol '|').

 For example, in the Title and Statement of Responsibility field:

245 14 $aThe Viking dig :$bexcavations at York /$cRichard Hall.

> *$a introduces the title proper*
> *$b introduces the other title information*
> *$c introduces the statement of responsibility.*

EXERCISE 3.4

Look closely at each of the MARC records, and answer the following questions.

1.

000		02834cam a2200445 i 4500
001		000052746235
008		140109s2014 enka b 001 0 eng c
020	__	$a9781472527578 (hbk.)
082	04	$a363.72801$223
100	1_	$aViney, William,$eauthor.
245	10	$aWaste :$ba philosophy of things /$cWilliam Viney.
264	_1	$aLondon :$bBloomsbury,$c2014.
300	__	$axi, 218 pages :$billustrations ;$c24 cm.
336	__	$astill image$bsti$2rdacontent
336	__	$atext$btxt$2rdacontent
337	__	$aunmediated$bn$2rdamedia
338	__	$avolume$bnc$2rdacarrier
504	__	$aIncludes bibliographical references (pages [203]-214) and index.
650	_0	$aRefuse and refuse disposal$xPhilosophy.
650	_0	$aRefuse and refuse disposal in literature.
650	_0	$aRefuse and refuse disposal in art.
650	_0	$aAntiquities$xPhilosophy.
650	_0	$aRuins in literature.
650_0		$aWaste (Economics) in literature.

a. What type of material is this?

b. What is the title?

c. Who is the author?

d. Is it illustrated?

e. Write down the ISBN.

f. What is this publication about?

2.

000   01167cem a2200361 i 4500

001   000052187138

008   131105s2013 flu a 1 eng

040   __ $aDLC$beng$cDLC$erda

050   00 $aG4284.S4 2013$b.A2

110   2_ $aAAA (Organization : U.S.)

245   10 $aSeattle, Washington /$cAAA.

250   __ $a2013/2014 edition.

255   __ $aScale 1:39,600. one in. equals approximately 0.62 miles or 1.01 km

264   _1 $aHeathrow, FL :$bAAA,$c[2013]

300   __ $a1 map :$bcolor ;$c119 x 89 cm, sheet 122 x 92 cm, folded to 23 x 11 cm.

336   __ $acartographic image$2rdacontent

337   __ $aunmediated$2rdamedia

338   __ $asheet$bnb$2rdacarrier

490   0_ $aCity series

500   __ $aIncludes inset and map of downtown Seattle.

500   __ $aIndexes, Seattle area map, and 2 local route maps on verso.

651   _0 $aSeattle (Wash.)$vMaps.

651   _0 $aSeattle Metropolitan Area (Wash.)$vMaps.

a. What type of material is this?

b. What is the title?

c. Is it colored or black and white?

d. Who produced it?

e. Is it part of a series? If so, what is the name of the series?

f. What is it about?

EXERCISE 3.5

Look at the following examples of catalog entries and answer the questions.

1.

TITLE	The gentleman's recreation : in four parts, viz. hunting, hawking, fowling, fishing : wherein these ... exercises are largely treated of, and the terms of art for hunting and hawking more amply enlarged ... with an abstract at end of each subject of such laws as relate to the same ... with the addition of a Hunting-horse.
AUTHOR	Cox, Nicholas, fl. 1673-1721.
EDITION	3rd ed.
PUBLISHED	London : printed by Freeman Collins for Nicholas Cox, 1686.
DESCRIPT	4 pts. in 1 v. : 4 plates, ill. ; 19 cm.
SUBJECT	1) Fowling.
	2) Hunting.
	3) Falconry.
	4) Fishing.
	5) Forestry law and legislation -- Great Britain.
	6) Game-laws -- Great Britain.
NOTE(S)	Each part has special t.p. and separate pagination.
CONTENTS	With which is bound: G. Langbaine, The hunter. Oxford, 1685.

LOC'N	CALL #	STATUS
Petherick Reading Rm	799.2 COX	Not for loan

a. What type of material is described in this catalog entry?

b. Who is the author?

c. Who printed this item?

d. What is the date of publication?

e. Which edition is this publication?

f. Is it illustrated?

g. Does it include an index?

   h. What is this publication about?

   i.. How could you find other books on this subject?

   j. Which classification scheme does this library use?

   k. Why do you think this publication cannot be borrowed?

  2.

TITLE	The spirit of '45.
ALSO TITLED	Spirit of '45.
	Which side are you on? (Motion picture)
OTHER CREATORS	Loach, Ken, 1936-, (film director.)
PUBLISHED	[Great Britain] : Dogwoof, 2013.
COPYRIGHT	© 2013
PHYSICAL DESCRIPT	videodiscs (PAL, 512 min.) : DVD video sound, color and black and white ; 4 3/4 in. + 1 folded sheet (4 pages ; illustrations, 18 cm)
SUBJECTS	Social change -- Great Britain -- History -- 20th century.
	Public welfare -- Great Britain -- History -- 20th century.
	Coal Strike, Great Britain, 1984-1985.
	Great Britain -- Politics and government -- 1945-1964.
	Great Britain -- Social conditions -- 20th century.
SUMMARY	'1945 was a pivital year in British history. The unity that carried Britain through the war allied to the bitter memories of the inter-war years led to a vision of a better society. The spirit of the age was to be our brother's and our sister's keeper. Director Ken Loach has used film from Britain's regional and national archives, alongside sound recordings and contemporary interviews to create a rich political and social narrataive. The Spirit of '45 hopes to illuminate and celebrate a period of unprecedented community spirit in the UK, the impact of which endured for many years and which may yet be rediscovered today.--Container.

LOC'N	CALL #	STATUS
Central library	DVD 941.085 SPIR	Available

a. What type of material is described in this catalog entry?

b. Who is the creator?

c. Who is the publisher of this item?

d. What is it about?

e. What is the playing time?

3.

TITLE	International journal of early childhood = Revue internationale de l'enfance préscolaire = Revista internacional de la infancia pre-escolar.

LIB. HAS Vol.1, n.1 (1969) to the present.

PUBLISHER	Dublin, Ireland : OMEP Publications, 1969-
PHYS DESCR	volumes : illustrations ; 25 cm.
FREQUENCY	Semiannual
NOTE	English, French, or Spanish, with summaries in the other two languages.
SUBJECT	Education, Preschool—Periodicals.
ISBN/ISSN	0020-7187
ADD AUTHOR	World Organization for Early Childhood Education

a. What type of material is described in this catalog entry?

b. When was the first issue of this publication published?

c. In what language is it published?

d. How would you find other items on the same topic/s?

EXERCISE 3.6

Answer the following questions using a library of your choice. (Use a large, general library if possible.)

1. How many items does the library hold by Nelson Mandela?

2. Does the library hold *Silent spring?* Where?

3. Does the library have any items on dress design?

4. How much material does the library hold on Virginia Woolf?

5. Does the library have anything on International Women's Year? Where?

6. Does the library subscribe to the popular news magazine *Time?* Where would I find it?

7. Does the library hold any items on practical politics?

8. How much material can you find on Pierre and Marie Curie?

9. Does the library have anything on Volvos? Where?

10. Does the library have any sound recordings of Dame Joan Sutherland? If so, what are they?

EXERCISE 3.7

Answer the following questions using a library of your choice. (Use a large, general library if possible.)

1. Which of the following could you look for in your library's catalog and why?
    a. Does the library receive *Scientific American*?

    b. Does the library have a copy of *Travels with Charley*?

    c. Is there an article about robots in *Life magazine*?

    d. Does the library have any DVDs on occupational health and safety?

    e. Where would I find a recent article by Ita Buttrose?

2. What name is used in the catalog for:
    a. Louisa M. Alcott

    b. IRS (Internal Revenue Service)

    c. National Gallery of Modern Art (Italy)

    d. NASA

    e. Guggenheim Museum

CHAPTER FOUR
Copy Cataloging

Introduction

When libraries describe their resources in a standardized way (using descriptive cataloging guidelines such as RDA) and encode them in a standard communication format (such as MARC) they are able to share their bibliographic records with other libraries. Sharing bibliographic records is common when one library buys a resource that has already been obtained and described by another library. The process of searching for an existing bibliographic record and replicating it for your library catalog is called **copy cataloging**.

The purpose of this chapter is to explain the steps that are involved in copy cataloging rather than teach you how to catalog. Cataloging procedures are quite complex and need to be studied separately. If you would like to learn how to catalog, you will find the procedures in *Learn cataloging the RDA way* by Lynn Farkas and Helen Rowe.

What is Copy Cataloging?

In simple terms, copy cataloging is the process of cataloging resources using already existing bibliographic records.

More specifically, copy cataloging involves:
- finding an existing bibliographic record that matches the item in hand
- editing the record to improve or upgrade the information it contains
- attaching appropriate holdings information to the bibliographic record, including location, classification and circulation status.

Copy cataloging allows library staff to catalog faster and therefore make their resources available for clients more quickly and easily.

When a library cannot catalog a resource making use of existing records, cataloging staff need to create original catalog records. Original cataloging is the process of creating new bibliographic records (in a standardized way, to enable sharing). Original cataloging places a heavier demand on staff time and takes longer than copy cataloging, so materials are not ready for patrons to use as quickly.

The Copy Cataloging Process

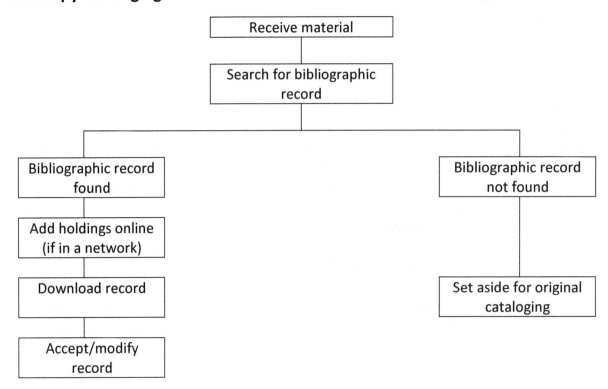

Sources of Copy Cataloging Records

There are several options for obtaining copy cataloging records, including:

- manual copy cataloging by finding a record in another catalog. Once found, these records can either be downloaded, or copied and pasted into your library's catalog
- using Cataloging in Publication (CIP) records
- using catalog subscription services that find or create records and sell them to libraries. These services are provided on a commercial basis, offering original and copy cataloging
- purchasing MARC records when you purchase resources from suppliers
- copying a record from a network or consortium that your library belongs to, like OCLC, Libraries Australia, etc.
- 'triggering' an automatic download by adding your holdings to a record.

Manual Copy Cataloging

Library staff find a record in another catalog, and either download it, or copy and paste it into their library catalog, editing the information as required.

The advantages of this are:

- Records have usually been cataloged by experienced catalogers so will be of a higher quality.
- Fuller records are available so all the information you need should already be in the record.
- Libraries that don't catalog many resources, or that cannot afford to subscribe to a large database or subscription service, can access bibliographic records.

Disadvantages:
- It may take time to find the record on another library's OPAC or in a union catalog.
- It could take as long as doing the original cataloging if the record needs to be edited.
- You may need to modify the record to suit your local requirements.

Cataloging in Publication (CIP)

Cataloging in Publication (CIP) is a service offered by national libraries to create metadata for resources published in their country. A Cataloging in Publication record (also known as CIP data) is a bibliographic record prepared before the book is published and included on the copyright page, which helps libraries and book dealers with their book processing.

Advantages
- Bibliographic records that libraries can use in their catalogs have already been created.

Disadvantages
- CIPs are sometimes brief because often they are created from a summary provided by the publisher and don't include all the details expected in a full catalog record.
- Changes can occur between the creation of the CIP and the time of the publication of the resource.
- CIP records may require some editing to reflect last minute changes made to information within the resource or on its packaging.

EXERCISE 4.1

Visit the Cataloging in Publication Program page on the British Library's website, http://www.bl.uk/bibliographic/cip.html; the Library of Congress' website, http://www.loc.gov/publish/cip/; or the National Library of Australia's website, http://www.nla.gov.au/cip.

1. How does the CIP Program work?

2. What is the purpose of the CIP Program?

3. Who is eligible for the CIP Program?

Other sources of copy cataloging include:
- catalog subscription services
- purchasing MARC records when you purchase resources from suppliers
- copying a record from a network or consortium
- automatic download triggered by adding your holdings to a record.

Catalog Subscription Services

Catalog subscription services search databases of records that can be downloaded into an integrated library system (ILS) for a fee. They may charge a set annual fee or there may be a membership fee with an additional charge for every record searched and downloaded. Depending on where the subscription service gets its records, the standard of cataloging can vary. Some services use a credit system for those libraries prepared to share their records to reduce their download fee, and some hire professional catalogers to input just for their database.

Advantages:
- The hit rate for records can be high as the search database is large.
- The service is quick, and usually supported.
- It is Internet based, so it can be globally supported.
- The protocols used can be modified for an individual ILS.

Disadvantages:
- The fees can be quite high.
- The speed at which items are cataloged can sometimes be delayed due to the volume of resources and records.
- Smaller libraries may not use enough records so may not get value for money.

Purchasing MARC Records When You Purchase Resources from Suppliers

A number of book vendors offer libraries the option of purchasing MARC bibliographic records along with the resources they buy.

Advantages:
- Bibliographic records are available for download for each of the resources that are purchased.
- An account has already been set up with the supplier.
- There is consistency in the records that are received as the resources are cataloged by one company.

Disadvantages:
- The library is limited to the resources and records the supplier can provide.
- You are locked in to the prices the supplier asks.

Copying a Record from a Network or Consortium

If you belong to a network or consortium, you can search across all the records contained in its union catalog. When you find the record for your resource, you can download it into your ILS, editing any information as required.

Advantages:

- Many records are available, and each record is a 'free' download.
- A search can be conducted on similar libraries to increase the likelihood of finding bibliographic records.
- In large networks, international records are often available to download.

Disadvantages:

- Records need to be checked and possibly modified before being uploaded into your ILS.
- There may be inconsistencies in the cataloging, if you use records created by a range of other libraries.

Trigger an Automatic Download by Adding your Holdings to a Record

Adding, editing or deleting holdings in some union catalogs will automatically trigger a download of that updated bibliographic record into your library's ILS.

Advantages

- The download of bibliographic records happens automatically.
- It is not necessary to add bibliographic records twice (i.e., once in the union catalog and once in the library's catalog).

Disadvantages

- In some systems, time and skill is needed to set up parameters to make automatic downloads happen.

How To Copy Catalog

1. Search the library's catalog for a bibliographic record that matches the item to be cataloged.
   a. Search standard numbers (e.g., ISBN/ISSN/Control number)
   OR
   b. Search title (if no record was found with the standard number search)

2. If a catalog record is found:
   a. check that the copy cataloging record and the item in hand are the same
      Same title and author
      same date of publication and/or edition
      same record control number (e.g., LC number from CIP, or ISBN/ISSN)

    b. If all these fields match

        Check the correctness of the copy for:

           1. descriptive cataloging

           2. classification number

           3. subject headings

        Accept the copy; or modify it to suit the needs of your library

        Attach holdings information for the new resource.

3. If no record is found, search another source such as a union catalog (like OCLC, WorldCat, Library of Congress), using the same process as in Steps 1 and 2 above.

4. If a record is not found in any catalog, set the resource aside for original cataloging.

 When you select a bibliographic record to copy catalog, it must match the resource you wish to catalog in its form, its content and its publication details. On a MARC record you will need to match the following MARC tags with the resource:

Must match: Field	Description
020/022 (if present)	ISBN/ISSN
245	Title Statement
250 $a	Edition Statement
264 $b	Publication, Distribution, etc.
300	Physical Characteristics
4XX $a (if present)	Series Statement

A word of warning. You will need to create new catalog records if you have:

- copies of the same resource in print, as an e-book and in microfilm. These would need three separate records – one for each format of the resource
- a new edition – as there would be differences in the content of the resource
- a new publisher – even if everything else about the resource was the same, a new publisher would have different publication details.

EXERCISE 4.2

Here are some title pages and versos for a number of resources. From the two catalog records shown for each resource, choose which record would be the correct one to select when copy cataloging. Why did you choose this record?

1.

<table>
<tr>
<td>
Jones & Bartlett Learning
2015
</td>
<td>
World Headquarters
Jones & Bartlett Learning
5 Wall Street
Burlington, MA 01803

Fourth Edition
ISBN 9781284036695

Copyright © 2015 by Jones & Bartlett Learning, LLC, an Ascend Learning Company

All rights reserved
</td>
</tr>
</table>

1a.

```
000  02032cam a2200421 i 4500
008  130710s2015   maua    b    001 0 eng
010  __  $a 2013027707
020  __  $a 9781284036695
040  __  $a DNLM/DLC $c DLC $e rda $d DLC
042  __  $a pcc
050  00  $a TX361.A8 $b .F56 2015
082  00  $a 613.2024796 $2 23
100  1_  $a Fink, Heather Hedrick, $e author.
245  10  $a Practical applications in sports nutrition / $c Heather Hendrick Fink, Alan
         E. Mikesky.
250  __  $a Fourth Edition.
264  _1  $a Burlington, MA : $b Jones & Bartlett Learning, $c 2015
300  __  $a xxvi, 546 pages : $b illustrations ; $c 28 cm.
336  __  $a text $2 rdacontent
337  __  $a unmediated $2 rdamedia
338  __  $a volume $b nc $2 rdacarrier
504  __  $a Includes bibliographical references and index.
650  12  $a Nutritional Physiological Phenomena.
650  12  $a Sports $x physiology.
650  22  $a Exercise $x physiology.
700  1_  $a Mikesky, Alan E., $e author.
```

1b.

```
000 03797cam a2200493 a 4500
008 120116s2012   maua   b   001 0 eng d
010 __  $a 2011012887
020 __  $a 9781449646431
040 __  $a DLC $c DLC $d YDX $d OOJ $d YDXCP $d CDX
050 00  $a TX361.A8 $b F56 2012
082 00  $a 613.2024796 $2 22
100 1_  $a Fink, Heather Hedrick.
245 10  $a Practical applications in sports nutrition / $c Heather Hedrick Fink, Alan E.
            Mikesky, Lisa A. Burgoon.
246 30  $a Sports nutrition
250 __  $a 3rd ed.
260 __  $a Burlington, MA : $b Jones and Bartlett Learning, $c c2012.
300 __  $a xxi, 568 p. : $b ill. ; $c 28 cm.
504 __  $a Includes bibliographical references and index.
650 _0  $a Athletes $x Nutrition.
650 _0  $a Exercise $x Physiological aspects.
700 1_  $a Mikesky, Alan E.
700 1_  $a Burgoon, Lisa A.
```

2.

	Penguin Group (Australia) 707 Collins Street Melbourne, VIC 3008, Australia PO Box 23360, Melbourne VIC 3008 ISBN 9780670078783 Copyright © 2015 All rights reserved

2a.
000 00745cam a2200253 a 4500
008 140225s2013   enka   b   001 0 eng d
020 __ $a 9780987564405
020 __ $a 0987564404
040 __ $a QPPL
082 04 $a 641.3/02 $2 23
100 1_ $a Macri, Irena.
245 10 $a Eat drink paleo cookbook / $c Irena Macri.
260 __ $a [Great Britain] : $b I. Macri, $c [2013]
300 __ $a 217 p. : $b col. ill. ; $c 25 cm.
500 __ $a Cover title.
504 __ $a Includes bibliographical references and index.
650 _0 $a Cooking (Natural foods)
650 _0 $a Health.
655 _7 $a Cookbooks. $2 lcgft

2b.
000 00917cam a22003018i 4500
008 141007s2015   vra   000 0 eng d
020 __ $a 9780670078783 : $c $34.99
040 __ $a ANL $b eng $e rda $d ANL
042 __ $a anuc
082 04 $a 641.5637 $2 23
100 1_ $a Macri, Irena, $e author.
245 10 $a Eat drink Paleo cookbook / $c Irena Macri.
264 _1 $a Melbourne, Vic. : $b Penguin Group (Australia), $c 2015.
300 __ $a 217 pages : $b color illustrations ; $c 25 cm.
336 __ $a text $2 rdacontent
337 __ $a unmediated $2 rdamedia
338 __ $a volume $2 rdacarrier
650 _0 $a High-protein diet $v Recipes.
650 _0 $a Reducing diets $v Recipes.
650 _0 $a Diet therapy.
650 _0 $a Prehistoric peoples $x Nutrition.

3.

<table>
<tr><td></td><td>

Prestel Head Office
Prestel Verlag • Verlagsgruppe Random House GmbH
Neumarkter Straße 28
81673 München
Germany
UK Office
Prestel Publishing Ltd.
14-17 Wells Street
London W1T 3PD
USA Sales and Marketing Office
Prestel Publishing
900 Broadway, Suite 603
New York, NY 10003

ISBN-13: 9783791348070

Copyright © 2013
All rights reserved

</td></tr>
</table>

Other information: 223 pages, height 26 cm.

3a.
000 02365cam a2200445 a 4500
001 000051862327
003 AuCNLKIN
005 20140903110327.0
008 121008s2013   gw abc   000 0 eng d
020 __ $a 9783791348070
040 __ $a YDXCP $c YDXCP $d BTCTA $d UKMGB $d OCLCQ
050 _4 $a TR99 $b .H66x 2013
082 04 $a 779.095 $2 23
100 1_ $a Hooton, Keiko S.
245 10 $a Contemporary photography in Asia / $c Keiko S. Hooton, Tony Godfrey.
264 _1 $a Munich : $b Prestel, $c 2013.
300 __ $a 223 pages : $b illustrations (chiefly colored), map, ports. ; $c 26 cm.
336 __ $a text $2 rdacontent
337 __ $a unmediated $2 rdamedia
338 __ $a volume $2 rdacarrier
504 __ $a Includes bibliographical references.
650 _0 $a Photography $z Asia.
650 _0 $a Photography, Artistic.
651 _0 $a Asia $v Pictorial works.
700 1_ $a Godfrey, Tony.

3b.
000 02365cam a2200445 a 4500
008 121008s2013   gw abc   000 0 eng d
020 __ $a 9783791348070
100 1_ $a Hooton, Keiko S.
245 10 $a Contemporary photography in Asia / $c Keiko S. Hooton, Tony Godfrey.
264 _1 $a New York : $b Prestel, $c 2013.
300 __ $a 223 pages : $b illustrations (chiefly colored), map, ports. ; $c 26 cm.
336 __ $a text $2 rdacontent
337 __ $a unmediated $2 rdamedia
338 __ $a volume $2 rdacarrier
504 __ $a Includes bibliographical references.
700 1_ $a Godfrey, Tony.

 In summary:
- All incoming records must be an exact match for the resource.
- If in doubt as to whether a bibliographic record is an acceptable match, ask your supervisor.
- Do not import a record if that record is already in your catalog.

Editing Copy Cataloging Records

Common reasons for editing records when copy cataloging are:
- There are transcription errors, e.g., misspelling, or the number of pages is incorrect
- Some information is missing, such as the statement of responsibility or publication details
- ISBD punctuation is missing or incorrect
- local policy is to use the current descriptive cataloging guidelines (RDA) but the record was created using the old cataloging rules (AACR2)
- local policy is to include access points for all authors but the record does not include them all
- local policy is to include at least one subject heading but there are none in the record

Upgrading copy cataloging records requires attention to detail. It takes more time to catalog a resource but adds value to the catalog and makes the catalog a more effective tool for users.

EXERCISE 4.3

Look at the OPAC records displayed below. Identify what is wrong with each of these records.

1.

Author:	Coombes, Allen J.
Title	The A to Z of plant names : a quick reference guide to 4000 garden plants / Allen J. Coombs.
Edition:	1st ed.
Published:	Portland, Or. : Timber Press, c2012.
Description:	312 pages ; 22 cm.
ISBN:	9781604691962
Notes:	Includes bibliographical references (p. 341-342)
Subjects:	Plants -- Great Britain -- Nomenclature -- Dictionaries.
	Plants -- North America -- Nomenclature -- Dictionaries.
	Botany -- Great Britain -- Dictionaries.
	Botany -- North America -- Dictionaries.

2.

Author:	Hay, Sam, (author).
Title:	Undead pets : Rise of the zombie rabbit and Flight of the battered budgie / by Sam Hay ; read by Toby Longworth.
Also titled:	Rise of the zimbie rabbit
	Flight of the battered birdie
Content type:	spoken word.
Carrier type:	audio disc.
Edition:	Complete & unabridged.
Published:	Bath, England : AudioGO, 2013.
Description:	pages : CD audio, digital ; 12 cm.
ISBN:	9781471362590
Series:	Chivers CD children's audio books
Contents:	Rise of the zombie rabbit -- Flight of the battered budgie.
Performer:	Reader : Toby Longworth.
Subjects:	Talking books for children.
	Rabbits -- Juvenile fiction.
	Dogs -- Juvenile fiction.
	Budgerigar -- Juvenile.
	Zombies -- Juvenile fiction.
Other authors:	Longworth, Terry, (narrator).

3. See the title page below and check whether this record is correct.

Author: Lahti, Arto.
Title: Globallization and Afican economics / Arto Lahti.
Content type: text.
Media type: unmediated.
Carrier type: volume.
ISBN: 9789526041834 (pbk.)
                   9789526041841 (pdf)
LC call number:HF1611
Series: Business + economy
Notes: Includes bibliographical references.
Subjects: Globalization -- Africa.
                   Africa -- Foreign economic relations.
                   Africa -- Economic conditions.

Other information: 93 pages and 30 cm high

Procedure for Adding Extra Copies

These procedures are used when adding additional copies to an existing catalog record:

- Check the catalog for the existing record, using the match points described earlier.
- Confirm the item is not a new edition with the same title. (If it is a new edition you will need to create a new record for this edition, not attach it to the record of a previous edition).
- Write the bibliographic record number and/or call number in the appropriate position on the item.
- Add the number of copies to the bibliographic record, if this is a practice in your library.
- Send the item for final processing.

REVISION QUIZ 4.4
Use the following questions to revise your understanding of copy cataloging procedures. You do not need to write down all the answers.

1. What is the difference between original cataloging and copy cataloging?

2. List three ways of obtaining records for copy cataloging.

3. List tasks library technicians may perform in a cataloging department.

4. List the basic steps followed when copy cataloging.

Levels of Cataloging Work

Original cataloging was once regarded as a professional activity in libraries—that is, it was done by qualified librarians, and library technicians usually did copy cataloging and catalog maintenance.

This has changed as the skills of library technicians have been increasingly recognized.

Libraries also differ, and individual interests and skills as well as the pressures of work are factors in the allocation of responsibilities.

ACTIVITY 4.5

Thinking about the library where you work, or that you use regularly, put a tick next to each activity listed that is performed in libraries by the level of person specified. You will find that many activities are carried out by more than one level of staff.

ACTIVITIES	Librarian	Library Technician	Clerical Assistant	P/T Help (e.g., students)
1. Establishes policies and procedures				
2. Supervision				
3. Does original cataloging				
4. Performs bibliographic checking for access points				
5. Solves difficult bibliographic checking problems				
6. Catalogs material with cataloging information available				
7. Locates records in catalogs				
8. Does descriptive and subject cataloging on problem material				
9. Checks cataloging				
10. Catalogs by comparing with existing catalog records				
11. Checks cataloging using existing catalog records				
12. Checks entry of cataloging data				
13. Prepares books for circulation				
14. Supervises book preparation				
15. Maintains authority files				

CHAPTER FIVE
Circulation Systems

Introduction

Circulation refers to the process of lending materials from the collection to registered borrowers. A circulation module in an integrated library system (ILS) keeps track of various circulation transactions:

check-out:	assign a loan period and allow the user to keep the item during that period
check-in:	return materials on or before a specified date
renew:	extend the loan period and assign a new due date
place holds:	create a queue for an item already in use
manage fees:	pay overdue fines

Circulation work is quite complex and requires a system that can pull together a great deal of information each time an item is borrowed. Typical circulation systems are able to:

- confirm that the borrower is a registered client and is eligible to borrow materials
- differentiate between types of borrowers and lend items according to the type of borrower
- calculate loan periods based on the type of material, and the category of borrower
- keep track of how many items a client currently has on loan and impose a maximum they can borrow
- indicate when items are on loan and when they are due to be returned
- bring overdue items to the library's attention for recall purposes
- hold circulated items for other borrowers and inform them when the items are available.

Many integrated library software systems include circulation services that enable library clients to help themselves. For example, through the online catalog users can:

- list all the materials they currently have on loan and the related due dates
- extend the loan period for library materials if they are not on hold for someone else
- receive a reminder that items are coming due, via email or text message or a telephone call, a few days in advance
- place a hold on an item already on loan to another client
- receive an email message when an item that has a status of 'on order' in the catalog is ready to be used.

How these services are used can differ depending on whether clients visit the circulation desk or log on to the library system from a remote site.

Customer Relations

In many cases, a library user's first impression is based on their interaction with staff on the circulation desk. Clients judge libraries on the attitudes and efficiency of staff they encounter and often the outcome of these interactions determine whether they will return to the library. Prompt and professional service that takes cultural differences into account is an important part of all library service, and especially circulation service.

Staff should be:
- friendly
- helpful
- impartial
- informative
- but not overwhelming.

Staff should be particularly aware of the importance of treating clients impartially. Bending the rules for one client will result in demands from others for the same treatment. Being harsh with some may lead to a perception of discrimination.

Keep in mind that expectations and behaviors are strongly influenced by a person's cultural background. Even simple things like whether someone prefers a formal or casual greeting are culturally-specific. Be aware that your language or behavior may be unfamiliar or unexpected. Patience and tolerance go a long way in bridging cultural differences.

All libraries have rules and policies, but they also tend to have an informal policy on how rules are applied. Some libraries are strict in the interpretation of rules, and others are more lenient. Your treatment of clients should be consistent with the treatment provided by other staff members.

Borrower Registration

Most public libraries and publicly supported academic libraries allow anyone to use the collection onsite. However, libraries require clients to present personal identification and register if they wish to take items offsite. The borrower is then issued a paper or plastic card with a barcode, and allowed to check out materials.

Libraries normally restrict the use of their circulation services to certain client groups. For example, a school library serves its staff and students. Libraries may lend to other groups, but often charge a fee or require a deposit. For example, educational institutions lending to the public often demand a user fee from these external borrowers.

EXERCISE 5.1

Fill in the table to show the client groups of each type of library.

Type of library	Client group
Public library	
School or college library	
National library	
Special library	

The Registration Procedure

1. Determine whether the client is eligible for membership and what particular type of membership.
2. Establish whether the client has the necessary proof of eligibility and proper identification.
3. Ensure that the client understands the conditions of membership, such as deposits and fees.
4. Have the client fill in a registration form on paper or online; if paper, input this information into the ILS circulation module.
5. Provide the client with a card as proof of eligibility to borrow materials.
6. Explain the **borrowing limits** including:
   - number and type of items
   - loan period
   - fine policy.
7. If available, provide a handout describing the services and/or a list of opening hours, or suggest attending a tour.

1. Eligibility for Membership

When the client first requests registration, you must determine if he or she is in one of the eligible client groups. This involves requesting documentation that identifies his or her status and explaining the various categories of borrowers.

Libraries give different borrowing privileges to different types of clients. Certain types of clients may be able to:

- borrow certain kinds of material while others may not (e.g., adults may borrow DVDs but children may not)
- borrow for different lengths of time (e.g., teachers may borrow serial issues for three weeks and students for one week)
- be exempt from fines while others are not (e.g., senior citizens may be exempt from fines in a public library)
- borrow larger or smaller numbers of items
- renew items more or less often than others
- be given priority for the use of material (e.g., having items recalled from other borrowers when they request them).

For example, a typical educational institution might offer these differing services to clients:

Patron category	Material type	Item limit	Loan period	Renewals allowed	Overdue fines
Students	Books & DVDs	20	14 days	2	$5 per week
Students	Books on Reserve	3	3 hours	no	$1 per hour
Faculty	Books & DVDs	No limit	100 days	2	No fines
Students & Faculty	Laptops, headphones, calculators	3	4 hours	1	$10 per hour
Staff	Books & DVDs	No limit	21 days	2	No fines
Students from other schools	Books (excluding Reserve)	5	7 days	no	$5 per week
General public	Books (excluding Reserve)	2	7 days	no	$20 per week

A public library may structure their borrowing parameters based solely on material type:

Item	Loan Period
Books	21 days
DVDs (except language learning DVDs)	7 days
Language learning DVDs (including literacy)	21 days
Periodicals & magazines	7 days
Music scores	21 days
Photographs & maps	7 days
Digital equipment	3 hours

 EXERCISE 5.2

Look at the website of two different types of libraries in your area. Fill in the tables below to show the client groups they serve and the different privileges given to the different client groups.

Library name & type:

Patron category	Material type	Item limit	Loan period	Renewals allowed	Overdue fines

Library name & type:

Patron category	Material type	Item limit	Loan period	Renewals allowed	Overdue fines

2. Necessary Proof of Eligibility/Identity

Usually, proof of identity is required when a client wants to be registered. Library policy outlines acceptable proof of identification; this may differ for each client group. For example, school libraries often obtain a list of students and staff from administrative records, or upload their names to the ILS in batches at the beginning of the academic term.

In a typical public library, proof of identification for the various client groups might be:

Client group	Identification required
Adults 18 years old +	Driver's license Evidence of paying property taxes to the county or municipality Other photo ID with home address
Children	Parent or guardian photo ID and signature on the registration form
Senior citizens	Same as adults, plus ID proving status (such as senior's card, health care card, veteran's card, etc.)
Special groups such as housebound, visually impaired	Letter of introduction from physician, community nurse, etc.
Non-resident adult	Driver's license Other photo ID with home address

ACTIVITY 5.3
Verify the registration policies of different libraries in your area.

Type of library	Identification required
School library	
College library	
Special library	

3. Ensure the Client Understands Conditions

Conditions might include limits on the number or type of materials borrowed, or a deposit or nonrefundable fee required before registration is completed.

It is important to ensure that the client understands these conditions. For example, if public clients of a university library are charged a fee, make certain that they are aware it is a nonrefundable annual fee. Explain that it is not a deposit that is returnable when clients cancel their membership and that it excludes access to some library materials such as the reserves collection.

4. Registration

A registration form collects all necessary information about the client, including name and contact information for correspondence and overdue notices. This information is stored in the client's patron record in the library system. Paper registration forms are usually not kept after being entered into the circulation module unless there is a need for a signature proving that the client agrees to certain conditions.

Academic libraries often batch upload patron data from the university registrar into their ILS. Some libraries allow patrons to apply online, and once approved, mail the library card to their home address or issue it on the spot.

Here is a sample borrower registration form.

LOS ANGELES PUBLIC LIBRARY

LIBRARY CARD APPLICATION
SOLICITUD DE TARJETA BIBLIOTECARIA

APPROVED IDENTIFICATION IS REQUIRED. PLEASE PRINT. ALL INFORMATION IS CONFIDENTIAL.
ES NECESARIO PRESENTAR UN DOCUMENTO DE IDENTIFICACIÓN VÁLIDO. ESCRIBA EN LETRAS DE MOLDE.
TODA INFORMACIÓN ES CONFIDENCIAL.

Name / Nombre
(Begin with last name / empiece con su apellido)

Complete if 17 years or younger / *Conteste si tiene 17 años de edad o menos*

Age / Edad   0-11   12-17   Birth Date / *Fecha de nacimiento*
Month / Mes   Day / Dia   Year / Año

Parent's / Guardian's Name
Nombre del padre, madre o tutor legal
(Begin with last name / empiece con el apellido)

Address / Domicilio

City/State
Cuidad/Estado
Zip Code / Código postal

Phone Number
Número de teléfono

Cellular Provider*
Proveedor de
telefonía móvil

To receive hold notices by text, please provide your cell phone number and provider. If you do not want text messages, please provide a contact phone number, no provider. / *Si desea recibir mensajes de texto cuando sus reservas estén disponibles, proporcione su número de teléfono móvil y su proveedor de telefonía móvil. Si no desea recibir mensajes de texto, sólo incluya su número de teléfono.*

* You may be charged for text messages, depending on your cell phone service plan / *Su proveedor de telefonía móvil podría cobrarle cargos por recibir mensajes de texto.*

E-Mail Address / *Correo electrónico*

Mother's First Name
Primer nombre de su madre

I accept responsibility for all materials charged to this card with or without my consent. I agree to observe all library rules; to promptly pay all charges; and to notify the library of any changes to this information. I understand that I am the only person authorized to use my library card.

I understand that all library materials, including books, audiovisual items, electronic databases and the Internet (World Wide Web), are available to all library users. I understand that I am responsible for my child's use of all library materials, including the Internet.

Acepto que soy responsable de todos los materiales tomados prestados con esta tarjeta con o sin mi permiso. Me comprometo a cumplir con todos los reglamentos de la biblioteca, a pagar inmediatamente todos los cargos y a notificar a la biblioteca sobre cualquier cambio en la información suministrada en esta solicitud. Entiendo que soy la única persona autorizada para utilizar mi tarjeta de la biblioteca.

Entiendo que todos los materiales, incluidos libros, materiales audiovisuales, recursos electrónicos y la Internet, están a disposición de todos los usuarios de la biblioteca. Entiendo que soy responsable del uso que mis hijos hagan de los materiales de la biblioteca, incluida la Internet.

Signature of applicant **or** parent or guardian if applicant is 17 years or younger:
Firma del solicitante o del padre, madre o tutor legal si el solicitante tiene 17 años de edad o menos:

OFFICE USE ONLY

Barcode #27244   Agency   Date

5/11

(Reprinted with permission of Los Angeles Public Library)

This screenshot is an example of patron record creation in the circulation module of an ILS:

					Insert Patron Record · New PATRON	

File Edit View

Insert   Save/Cl...   Delete   Print   Cancel

New PATRON   Last Updated: 09-15-2014   Created: 09-15-2014   Revisions: 0

EXP DATE	08-31-2017	HOME LIBR	mcirc Circulation Desk	CUR ITEMB	0
PCODE1	s SESSIONAL	PMESSAGE		OD PENALTY	0
PCODE2	q QUEENS	MBLOCK	-	ILL REQUES	0
PCODE3	0 Unused	CL RTRND	0	CUR ITEMC	0
P TYPE	15 Faculty	MONEY OWED	$0.00	CUR ITEMD	0
TOT CHKOUT	0	BLK UNTIL	- -	CIRCACTIVE	- -
TOT RENWAL	0	CUR ITEMA	0	Notice Preference	
CUR CHKOUT	0				

➤ n Name:
➤ a   Address:

➤ t Telephone:
➤ z Email:
➤ b Barcode:
➤ =
➤ u University ID:

Record Creation Mode (INS)

Software copyright Innovative Interfaces, Inc. Used with permission

5. Provide Client with a Card

A borrower's card is given to the client as proof of lending privileges. Many libraries will not provide any service unless the client can produce the card. Other libraries will allow service if the client can prove their identity in some other way.

Cards are usually barcoded, making it easy to scan and quickly retrieve the patron record at the circulation desk or when the patron uses a self-checkout machine.

https://www.hkpl.gov.hk/en/about-us/services/borrower-reg/lc-for-school-children.html
Reprinted with permission

6. Explain Borrowing Limits and Services

Ensure that the client understands any borrowing limits as well as the fining policy of the library. Many libraries have a handout with this information and include it on their website.

Take advantage of this opportunity to provide a little public relations—an important facet of circulation work. Let the client know about the library's other services and where to ask for assistance. Library clients want to feel confident that your services are accessible and valuable.

Keeping Registration Up-to-Date

Registration is normally done for a specific period such as one calendar year (January - December) in public libraries or the academic year in school and university libraries. If the records are not batch uploaded and updated, clients may be asked to confirm their address or phone number so that their patron records can be checked for accuracy.

ACTIVITY 5.4
Obtain copies of the following from a library:

1. a registration form

2. a library card

3. a policy showing who is eligible for registration, what identification is required, and the possible categories of borrowers

4. library promotional material.

Circulation Services

Lending Items

The purpose of circulation systems is to keep track of the library materials on loan to registered borrowers, and to monitor their due dates. Many systems can be configured to send email or text messages to patrons a few days before items are due, to give them a reminder and decrease the chance they will forget and incur an overdue fine.

Sometimes a client's loan request is not permitted. The client may already have the maximum number of loans allowed or has asked for a type of material that cannot be loaned out. It is very important that all staff follow the policy of the library. If you must refuse a loan, give the reason politely: "I'm sorry but students are not allowed to borrow videos." Follow the library's loan policy and be consistent.

Renewals

Libraries expect clients who wish to use items for longer than the loan period to renew the loan and usually this is possible for patrons to do themselves online. Loans are normally extended unless another client has put a hold on the material. There may be a limit on the number of times a renewal is allowed to ensure that materials in demand are shared.

Fines

Many libraries impose fines when clients do not return material at the end of the loan period. Fines are used as an incentive to return items in order to make the collection available to as many people as possible.

On the other hand, fines can be a deterrent to returning material, or even to borrowing at all. Dealing with fines requires tact.

Short-Term Loans

Library materials that are in high demand are often shelved separately and have shorter loan periods. For example, material selected by teachers for their students is generally put 'on reserve' so that students can use the material for a few hours.

Holds

Library users might request that an item on loan be made available to them when it is returned. When the item is returned, the circulation system alerts staff (in the form of an audible beep, or a pop-up screen) that the item is On Hold. Staff can then set the item aside rather than send it for re-shelving. Either the staff member telephones or sends an email, or the circulation module sends a message to let the patron know the hold is ready to be collected.

A library may decide to display records in the catalog for titles that are on order, but not yet received. If this is the case, the library may also set the system to allow holds to be placed on these orders. When one of these items is received, the system alerts staff that a hold is attached. Staff can then send the item for cataloging and final processing. Once the item is cataloged and processed, the client is notified.

Missing Items

Items that disappear, as well as items that borrowers insist they have returned, must be shown as missing in the catalog. Often this is done by adding a note or code to the item record. Staff will check the shelves a number of times before the item is finally pronounced gone and either withdrawn from the catalog or replaced.

Banning

When clients persistently neglect to return items, refuse to pay for missing items, or have a large number of fines outstanding, they may be banned from using the library's collection. Banning is more common in academic libraries where it is vital that all students have equal access to collections. Banning is a last resort in most libraries, as it is considered bad public relations.

Using the Circulation Module in an ILS

Circulation modules vary, but some procedures are common to all of them. Most require passwords to login and have access to the functionality needed for a person's duties. For example, a circulation assistant might be allowed to search the catalog, checkout materials and check them back in, but may not be able to change any information in the records.

A barcode reader is used to scan the barcode on a library card and retrieve the patron record, and then scan the barcode on the item and retrieve the item record. The system then links the records and calculates a date due, based on the type of material and/or type of borrower. When items are returned, scanning the item barcode discharges the loan by removing the link to the patron record.

Barcode readers, particularly light pens, are notorious for not always reading the number. Often they still give a finishing 'beep', and it is easy to think the number has been accepted. Items are then left unrecorded, or recorded as overdue, when they are actually on the shelves. Therefore, it is always important to check the screen to confirm that the barcode was read and the check-in transaction completed.

In order to confirm the loan transactions and due dates, libraries can either send an email message, provide clients with a system-generated receipt that shows the date due, or manually stamp a date due slip inserted in the item to provide this information.

Most systems allow the circulation staff to decide whether illegal loans are to be allowed, rather than just refusing to process the loan. This decision process is referred to as overriding the system.

Some systems use function keys or macros to provide shortcuts from one task to another. It can be time-consuming for staff to have to move from one task to another by using menu commands or clicking a mouse. Learning shortcut keys and functions is an important part of using an automated system efficiently.

Some older systems have commands barcoded to allow quick movement from one process to another.

Circulation systems usually calculate fines upon return of the item and generally are able to print a receipt automatically when the fine has been paid. For accounting purposes, or to record proof of payment, these systems might also keep track of the fines paid by each borrower as well as the total of the fines collected. In academic libraries this data is forwarded to the registrar's office.

ACTIVITY 5.5

Visit a library and ask to observe as the following circulation transactions are completed:

1. Register a new borrower.

2. Lend him or her an item.

3. Discharge the item.

4. Place a hold on an item already on loan for a client.

5. Return the item on hold and notify the client who requested the reserve.

6. Return an overdue item. (Inform the client of the fine, collect the fine, and record payment on the system.)

ACTIVITY 5.6

Look at the circulation system used in your library, or choose a system from a vendor's website. Make a list of the shortcut functions available on the circulation system. You may need to look at the system manual to find them. Create a list that could be placed near the loan terminal for use by circulation staff.

Self-Checkout

Many libraries use self-checkout stations to save staff time checking out material and to reduce lines at the circulation desk. Clients position their barcoded library card and the barcodes of the items they wish to borrow under a barcode reader. The system then records the loans and desensitizes the security strips in the items. Clients who are ineligible to borrow for any reason will be referred to the staff at the circulation desk.

Some drawbacks to the use of self-checkout stations include:
- Automatic checkout may not be effective if barcodes and security strips are not positioned in the same place on all items.
- Libraries intending to introduce self-checkout may have to re-barcode some or all of their collections.
- The desensitizing machine can damage videos and software so they cannot be circulated this way.

Security Systems

Security systems are used to prevent material from being removed from the library without being properly checked out. Items have a magnetic strip placed inconspicuously in them. When the item is checked out, the strip is demagnetized as part of the process. If the strip has not been demagnetized, an alarm rings when the item passes between detection gates or barriers that are usually located near the exit. Strips are re-magnetized when the item is returned.

Some libraries pass the item around the barrier without demagnetizing the strips to save time and the expense of a demagnetizer. Clients collect the items when they have passed through the barrier. This can cause problems when the books are taken into other libraries or brought back into the lending library.

If the alarm is activated, do not assume that the client is stealing. Clothing tags, cell phones, items from other libraries, or security strips that have not been properly demagnetized might trigger alarms.

In the event of the alarm going off, here is a procedure to follow:

- Ask the client if he or she has any material from another library or is carrying something else that might have triggered the alarm.
- Politely request to check bags. (The client should open the bags, and staff should just observe.)
- Look for items that might have set off the alarm.
- Confirm that items from your own library are checked out and demagnetized.
- Explain that you may need to pass the material around the gate if, for example, it comes from another library that does not demagnetize items.
- Call for a supervisor if the client refuses to cooperate.

ACTIVITY 5.7

List the questions you would ask if a client set off the alarm on the security gate in your library. Practice asking these questions with a co-worker.

REVISION QUIZ 5.8
Use the following questions to revise your understanding of circulation. You do not need to write down all the answers.

1. Why do libraries distinguish among different categories of borrowers?

2. When do libraries keep the registration card that is filled in by the borrower?

3. What is a 'hold'? Choose the correct answer.
   a. The library agrees to keep a book from the shelves until the client picks it up.
   b. The library keeps a book for another client when it is returned from loan.
   c. A client requests a book that is on order in the catalog be held for him.
   d. The library puts a book into a special collection because it is in demand and only lends it for a short period.

4. Why is the attitude of circulation staff toward clients so important?

5. When checking out material, you are often given the choice of printing a receipt for all the items loaned out. What is the purpose of this slip?

6. Under what circumstances would a library consider re-barcoding some or all of the collection?

7. When would a borrower ask for a renewal?

8. Why do libraries fine clients for having items overdue?

Reserves

Also called Short-Term Loan, Closed Reserve or Short Loan, Reserve collections are primarily used in academic and school libraries where several library users want the same material at the same time. Required reading for a course or information needed to complete a particular assignment is often put on Reserve.

Many university libraries have a separate Short Loan or Reserve section in their libraries. Often material on Short Loan is not to be taken outside of the library.

In an academic library, reserve collections usually feature:
- loan periods as short as one day, or even just two hours
- material from the library's collection, personal copies from faculty, and temporary material such as photocopies
- heavy fines to discourage clients from keeping the item longer than permitted
- strict penalties if fines are not paid (e.g., withholding grades).

Special and public libraries may also have small collections of high-demand materials that are kept behind the service desk so that their use can be monitored.

Material for Reserve

In academic and school libraries, lecturers or teachers normally notify the library about resources that need to be placed on reserve. Sometimes all material on reading lists is automatically put here. To manage a reserve collection effectively, it is important to communicate with the teaching staff about their requirements and to ensure that library staff have enough time to process materials and make them available for circulation.

When the library does not have the material in the collection, teachers and lecturers sometimes put their own copies on reserve to make them available to students. Lecture notes and recordings are often kept on reserve. Articles may also be obtained via interlibrary loan for reserve collections.

In nonacademic libraries, material is generally put on reserve by library staff when they anticipate high demand.

Adding Material to Reserve Collections

Material in the library collection is put on reserve by:
- moving or copying the item record to the reserve system
- specifying the course for which the item has been put on reserve
- changing the call number in the item record and on the item itself to include the collection symbol
- re-shelving the material in a separate section of the library.

Material being added to the reserve collection is normally marked with large stickers or distinctive book jackets for easy identification by circulation staff.

For materials that are not part of the library collection, a temporary item record is created. Most automated circulation systems allow you to do this without having to add a full bibliographic record to the catalog.

Information on the relevant course is added to the record to allow staff to locate items that are requested by course name or number, or by the name of the lecturer. Students often do not have the citations of material they require; they only know that some material has been placed in the library for them.

Reserve Loans and Bookings

Varying loan periods can confuse staff and clients. To avoid this, many libraries offer only a few choices, such as 2-hour, 4-hour, or overnight loans. This policy also depends on the flexibility of the booking system.

Many booking systems allow students to reserve materials in advance in order to use them at particular times. This is done to give part-time students the same opportunity as full-time students to access material.

 This screenshot shows a booking for an item:

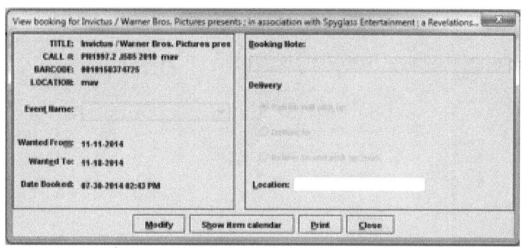

Software copyright Innovative Interfaces, Inc. Used with permission

If items are not returned to the reserve desk on time, another client is disadvantaged, so fines are heavy and no grace period is allowed. As with other library fines, grades are often withheld until fines are paid completely.

In public and special libraries, material on reserve is often only available on overnight loan or for use in the library only. This ensures that all clients have an equal opportunity to use the material.

EXERCISE 5.9

Consider a library where you are familiar with the short loan or reserve section.

1. List the issues for library staff in managing such a collection.

2. List the issues for library clients in using such a collection.

REVISION QUIZ 5.10

Use the following questions to revise your understanding of Reserves. You do not need to write down all the answers.

1. Why do libraries set up special short loan or reserve sections?

2. Name three differences between short loan conditions and normal loan conditions.

3. Where do the materials on reserve come from?

4. What types of libraries use a reserve system?

CHAPTER SIX
Interlibrary Loan

Introduction

Interlibrary loan (ILL) is the process of borrowing material from another library on behalf of a client. This service is known as interlibrary loan, but may also be called interloan, interlending, document delivery or document supply. When a library does not own a book or other piece of information that a client wants to use, ILL is an efficient way to meet the information need. Interlibrary loans allow libraries to provide their patrons with access to library collections all over the world, as well as share their own collections.

 ILL is a formal, reciprocal arrangement: libraries should be willing to do the work needed to lend materials in a timely way if they want to borrow from other libraries.

Interlibrary loans involve two separate processes – borrowing and lending.
- A borrowing library will request access to an item from a lending library.
- A lending library will fill the request either by providing access to the item or providing a reason why they cannot fill the request. Requests may be filled by:
    a. Lending the physical item for a period of time
    b. electronic delivery of an article or chapter, which the patron can keep
    c. photocopying, scanning or faxing, and delivering the article or chapter, which the patron can keep.

Interlibrary loan requests are most commonly processed electronically using systems based on the International Standard Organization's Interlibrary Loan Protocol (ISO ILL) Standards 10160 and 10161. The standards were created to allow computer systems—from different manufacturers, under different management, of different levels of complexity, and of different ages—to talk to each other. Libraries that follow these standards have an easier time sharing information about ILL transactions for both lending and borrowing activities.

Union Catalogs

A union catalog is a catalog that includes the collections of more than one library. Libraries around the world share details about the resources in their collections in various union catalogs. When a library adds a new title to their local catalog, they will either upload a copy of the bibliographic record to the union catalog or add their holdings symbol to an existing record in the union catalog. The result is a database that all members of the 'union' can search to verify which libraries hold a specific item.

The libraries that contribute their collections information into a shared union catalog may be grouped by geography (for example all libraries in a state or province) or by type of library (for example all academic libraries in a region).

Interlibrary loan systems work best when libraries use union catalogs that are current (new titles are added regularly and withdrawn titles are removed promptly) and full of standardized, accurate information.

Resource Sharing Networks

Most ILL networks are based on library type: for example, academic libraries tend to own the types of materials that other academic libraries want to borrow. Networks are also based on geography to save the time and expense of sending library materials across great distances.

Brief details of some of the resource sharing networks available around the world are provided below.

Australia

Libraries Australia Document Delivery (LADD) is Australia's largest interlibrary loan and document delivery service. It provides access to over 700 Libraries Australia libraries, the New Zealand TePuna interlibrary loan network and the international supplier Infotrieve. There are many other interlibrary loan networks and consortias operating in Australia, e.g., GratisNet (the collective of Australian health libraries), and GLASS (NSW & Victorian governmental libraries).

Britain

Britain has not established a formal national resource sharing framework. However, the British Library provides interlibrary loans through their British Library Document Supply Services (BLDSS). Britain also has Regional Library Systems that maintain union catalogs of the holdings of their member libraries and make resources available within their regional areas.

Canada

There is no centralized interlibrary loan service for the whole of Canada, but there are many ILL networks operating across the country. One example is the RACER system in Ontario which provides a one-search interface for all 21 university libraries in the province. RACER stands for Rapid Access to Collections by Electronic Requesting. ILL staff can track the status of requests and send emails to patrons informing them when requested items are available for pickup.

China

The National Library of China provides a centralized point for document delivery, interlibrary loan and international interlibrary loan to China, organizations inside and outside the country, general users and individuals. The Shanghai Library, together with a number of the university libraries in the country, has established the Shanghai Information Resources Consortium which offers interlibrary loan services.

Germany

Germany has a number of decentralized consortias to facilitate interlibrary loans within the country, including the German Interlibrary Loan and the Bavarian Library Network.

New Zealand
The New Zealand Interloan Scheme, Te Puna Interloan, is a cooperative for libraries to share their collections in New Zealand. The scheme is jointly administered by the Library and Information Association of New Zealand Aotearoa and the National Library of New Zealand.

South Africa
Sabinet provides access to the South Africa Catalog and offers online interlending requests through ReQuest. In recent years this has been supplemented by the OCLC platform of services.

United States
Interlibrary loan services operating in the United States are highly functioning, decentralized systems. Apart from those libraries that use OCLC, most state and regional library networks and consoritas have established their own interlibrary loan arrangements. Examples include Illinois Library and Information Network (ILLINET) which is a statewide library alliance representing the academic, public, school and special libraries that comprise Illinois' Regional Library Systems (RLS); and OhioLINK (Ohio Library and Information Network) which is a consortium of Ohio's college and university libraries and the State Library of Ohio.

OCLC
The OCLC (Online Computer Library Center) network uses WorldCat and WorldShare Interlibrary Loan to lend and borrow resources. Its purpose is to improve access to the information held in libraries around the globe, and find ways to reduce costs for libraries through collaboration.

WorldCat is a very large online public access catalog containing bibliographic records for the collections of approximately 72,000 libraries in 170 countries. The member libraries regularly upload their collection information, creating a valuable resource for ILL staff when they search for items requested by patrons.

Transnational Arrangements
Interlibrary loans are not limited to operation within one country. A number of formal transnational interlibrary loan arrangements have been established (e.g., Subito is the document delivery service of research libraries in Germany, Austria and Switzerland; Trans Tasman Interlending operates between Australia and New Zealand; Grupo Amigos and the Transborder Library Forum are transnational initiatives between Mexico and the United States).

Commercial Document Delivery Suppliers
A library might also contract the services of commercial document delivery suppliers who provide full-text articles, patents, government documents, and sometimes dissertations. This could be a fee-based service, as a supplement to resource sharing when no free versions are available.

Interlibrary Loan Codes

Interlibrary loan codes are general agreements on how interlibrary loans should be conducted. They set out the levels of service that are available and the rights and obligations of both borrowing and lending libraries (nationally and internationally).

The codes provide information on:

- definitions of interlending terminology
- procedures for making requests
- procedures for supplying requests (including loan periods, return of material, and renewals)
- urgent and priority requests
- charges and payment procedures (including payment of freight)
- steps taken to maintain client confidentiality
- care of material
- responsibilities for loss, damage and replacement.

Libraries are expected to make ILL requests only if they are consistent with the code for their country or network, unless other arrangements have been made in advance.

The International Federation of Library Associations and Institutions (IFLA) has prepared a set of principles and guidelines which may be used as the basis for any country's interlibrary loan code. The most recent edition of the IFLA *Model National Interlibrary Loan Code* is available at http://archive.ifla.org/VI/2/p3/model.htm. It is recommended as a model for all countries that do not at present have a national code for interlibrary loan, or that wish to revise their existing codes.

ACTIVITY 6.1
Some countries have national interlibrary loan codes, some have regional or consortia interlibrary loan codes. Working by yourself or in groups, compare another interlibrary loan code with the Australian Interlibrary Resource Sharing (ILRS) Code http://www.nla.gov.au/initiatives/ilrscode/index.html.

1. Do they have the same content?

2. What's different?

Limitations

Some libraries may lend resources but place restrictions on how they are to be used. For example, the item might be marked with the request 'for use in library only', 'no photocopying', or 'no renewals'. These restrictions should be adhered to by the library that receives the lent item.

Some libraries will lend most of their material but may not lend certain categories. Any limitations on lending will be determined by individual libraries. Items that may not be available for interlibrary loan could include:
- reference material
- short loan collection
- audio-visual material
- textbooks
- bound journals
- items in special or rare book collections
- manuscript material
- genealogy books
- dissertations
- theses.

It is a good idea to check whether the library will send these types of resources before you send a request for them.

Lending Policies

ILL staff may be asked to find the contact details and information on lending policies for a specific library before sending them an interlibrary loan request. Many national libraries maintain directories or databases of libraries in that country and links to their individual resource sharing policies. If someone in your country has compiled a directory of libraries, information about interlibrary loans may be included in it. This will allow you to see any special conditions, the charging policy and what service levels libraries provide.

For example the *Australian Interlibrary Resource Sharing (ILRS) Directory* available at http://www.nla.gov.au/ilrs/ lists all this information for Australian libraries.

EXERCISE 6.2

Check the lending policy and lending charges of two libraries near you.

1. What types of material don't they lend?

2. What charges do they make?

3. What priority services do they offer?

4. What methods can you use to pay them for ILL?

5. How can you send them requests?

Borrowing Procedures

These are the standard steps for borrowing items:

1. Verify bibliographic details and sources.
2. Ensure compliance with copyright legislation.
3. Prepare and transmit borrowing request.
4. Receive materials and notify client.
5. Return materials to lending library.

1. Verify Bibliographic Details and Sources

Before asking another library to lend you something, you must confirm that the item exists and that the bibliographic information is accurate. You can do this by finding it in an online database, authoritative bibliography, or index. Large online library catalogs are very useful for this, especially union catalogs that merge more than one library's holdings into one database (e.g., OCLC).

Remember to check your own library's catalog to ensure that you do not hold the resource before you request it from another library.

Searching and verifying bibliographic details is important for acquisitions, interlibrary loans, preparing bibliographies for clients, and other reference work. The following exercise will provide you with practice.

 EXERCISE 6.3
Answer the following questions using OCLC WorldCat http://worldcat.org or the Library of Congress catalog http://catalog.loc.gov. Begin by reading the Search or Help information to learn tips for effective searching.

1. Find the title of a book by Nadine Gordimer.

2. Find the title of a book about Nadine Gordimer.

3. Give the author and title of a book by Haruki Murakami.

4. Who wrote a criticism in English of Margaret Atwood's book *The handmaid's tale*? What is the title?

5. To which series does Mary Jane DeMarr's book about Barbara Kingsolver belong?

6. Find Thea Hayes' memoir about her life as a nurse. Transcribe the title and statement of responsibility.

7. When was Nelson Mandela born? When did he die?

8. What is the full title information for the book with ISBN 9780061733123?

9. Find a Braille version of *Cloudy with a chance of meatballs*. Who is the author? Who produced the Braille version?

2. Ensure Compliance with Copyright Legislation

It is the requesting library's responsibility to ensure that requests for copies of items conform to copyright law and that all necessary declarations and records are retained. This is an important aspect of interlibrary loan and should not be overlooked. A fuller discussion of copyright is provided later in this chapter.

3. Prepare and Transmit Borrowing Request

On every request, provide all bibliographic details, call numbers if known, contact details, level of service, and whether a loan or copy of the resource is required. As you determine where to place your requests, here are a few suggestions:

- use local resources first
- use libraries that also borrow from you
- use libraries that see their role as resource centers.

Interlibrary loan requests may be sent in the following ways:

- electronically via ILL networks such as OCLC, LADD, etc.
- by email or fax.

Using the interlibrary loan network, email or fax, you should prepare your request using a template. This serves as a form requiring all necessary details so that none are missed.

The telephone is not ideal for interlibrary loans because it interrupts the work of the receiving library. Information can be copied incorrectly, wasting staff time. Unless a previous agreement has been made, the telephone is usually not acceptable—even for very urgent requests. When the phone is used, the phone call should be followed by a request in one of the other formats listed above.

4. Receive Materials and Notify Client

Confirm that the received materials match your record of the request. Loans often arrive with an ILL transaction number from the lender or return address shipping labels. Keep these with your records.

Notify your client that the material has arrived and where it can be retrieved—usually the circulation desk or ILL office. Libraries might route the item to the client by courier or interdepartmental mail. Include a clear indication of the due date with the item, taking into account the time it will take to mail or courier it back to the lending library. Usually this is included on an ILL bookband like the one shown here.

Interlibrary Loan / Document Delivery
Shipping Book Band (Lending)

PLEASE DO NOT REMOVE THIS BOOKBAND

Supplying Library: Ryerson University, Library

Our ILL Responder #: 8016483

Courier Code:

Requesting Library: Bibliothèque Myriam et J.-Robert Ouimet
                      HEC Montréal

Your ILL Request #:   1539353

PICKUP AT:

For Your Patron:
Patron Category:

Title: Annual report, 1992-93
Author: Ontario Lottery Corporation
Article Title:

SPECIAL INSTRUCTIONS:

Loan Period: 3 weeks from the date of receipt with NO renewal.

No Renewals:
In Library Use Only:
No Photocopying:
Notes:

5. Return Materials to Lending Library

Items lent to patrons should be due back into your library a few days before the interlibrary loan return date, to give you time to process, package and return the loan to the lending library. Materials returned past the due date will likely incur fines as well as inconvenience the lending library. Materials should be sent back on time and in the same condition in which they were received.

Lending Procedures

These are the standard steps for lending items:

1. Receive and prioritize requests.
2. Decide if the library should accept the request by considering the consortium, state, or regional codes that apply, as well as the copyright laws.
3. Locate the item in the collection.
4. Copy/lend item, or items.
5. Send a report explaining why the item is not being loaned.
6. Record payment or debit the other library's account.
7. Package and send the item.
8. Receive items returned from ILL.

1. Receive and Prioritize Requests

Interlibrary loan requests arrive in the following ways:

- electronically via ILL networks such as OCLC, LADD, etc.
- by email or fax.

Determine the priority order of the requests based on your library's policy. For example, consortium agreements might specify that members' requests receive priority over other libraries.

Watch for requests that are marked 'Rush' or have 'Not wanted after' dates.

2. Should the Library Accept the Request?

In accepting the request, your library needs to decide:

- Does it conform to the ILL code?
- Does it breach copyright law?
- Is it something that your policy says you will lend?

You are not obliged to lend all items from your collection. Libraries may reject requests for high-use material, valuable or fragile material, reference material, or other specific collections. As previously noted, libraries are at liberty to determine the resources within their collection that may be withheld from interlibrary loan requests, or may have specific limitations placed on them.

Although it is the requesting library's responsibility to ensure that requests for copies of items conform to copyright law, the supplying library should not provide copies that are obviously in breach of the law.

Copyright laws differ in various countries, but in general libraries are permitted to copy material for another library if:

- the copy will not be used for commercial or business purposes. For example, copyright materials can be reproduced for use in the classroom
- the library collections are open to the public or the library collections are meant to serve the needs of students and researchers
- the copy includes a notice of copyright.

3. Locate the Item

Requests might arrive with call numbers included if the requesting libraries have looked them up in your online catalog. When the call number is supplied with the request, some libraries check the shelves first; others check all requests first in the catalog. It might save time to confirm that the item is not out on loan before going to the stacks to retrieve it. Items might be out for repair, missing, or in special collections. If a requested item is on loan and due to be returned in time to meet the request, you could put a hold on it.

The requesting library should be informed promptly if the request will be delayed or not supplied. The requesting library should include a 'date not required after' with the original request. If you cannot supply by that date, notify the requesting library immediately. If no date is given, assume the material will be required indefinitely.

4. Copy/Lend Items

Copying

Electronic scans or photocopies of articles from journals and chapters from books are usually sent with the understanding that they will not be returned. This service is called document delivery and may be subject to a per item fee.

Copying library materials should be done with care:

- Do not damage items by forcing spines flat
- Copy carefully so that the copy is readable and the edges of paragraphs are visible
- Include all pages
- Use sufficient exposure to ensure legibility.

Lending Materials

Items being loaned should be checked out through the circulation system so that local staff and clients know they are currently not available. Loan periods for ILL should take transit time as well as patron use time into account.

5. Send a Report Explaining Why the Item is Not Being Loaned

If for any reason you are unable to fulfil a request, reply promptly so the requesting library knows to ask elsewhere. You may not be able to supply a requested item for numerous reasons, including:

- item is at the bindery
- item is in process
- item is currently on loan
- item is lost
- item is non circulating

- item is not on the shelf
- item is not owned
- item is on hold
- item is on order
- item is on reserve
- item is in poor condition
- item was not found as cited
- there is a policy problem
- interlibrary loan request lacks copyright compliance
- preferred delivery time is not possible
- prepayment is required for the loan
- requested delivery service (e.g., a particular courier or a rush loan) is not supported
- volume and issue are not yet available for loan.

6. Record Payment

ILL networks use online systems to send and receive requests, keep track of transactions and process payments.

Some libraries form partnerships to lend and borrow among their consortia, or with similar types of libraries, without charging fees. They do this on a reciprocal arrangement, expecting that the other library will not charge them fees. Other libraries charge a lending fee to offset the staff and resource costs of providing ILL.

If your library charges other libraries a lending fee, you might need to send a monthly invoice or debit a deposit account. Some networks, like Libraries Australia Document Delivery, do this automatically for their members.

7. Package and Send the Item

Material for loan may be sent via an overnight courier, postal delivery, registered mail, or some other reasonably secure carrier, or the borrowing library could collect the resource from the lending library.

Loans are put in wrappers identifying the lending library and the conditions of loan, such as for in-library use only. Many libraries include a return address sticker to ensure the item is returned to the correct address. Padded bags are used to prevent damage.

A copy of the request should be sent with the loan for easy identification.

8. Receive Returned Items

Upon return, items must be discharged in the circulation system and reshelved. The lending library might receive a credit note or have funds transferred into an account, as payment for loans. ILL records should be updated and moved to a completed file. Libraries might use the completed file to compile annual statistics, monitor the costs of participating in ILL, and report income generated by fees and late fines.

This diagram shows the steps involved in the interlibrary loan process.

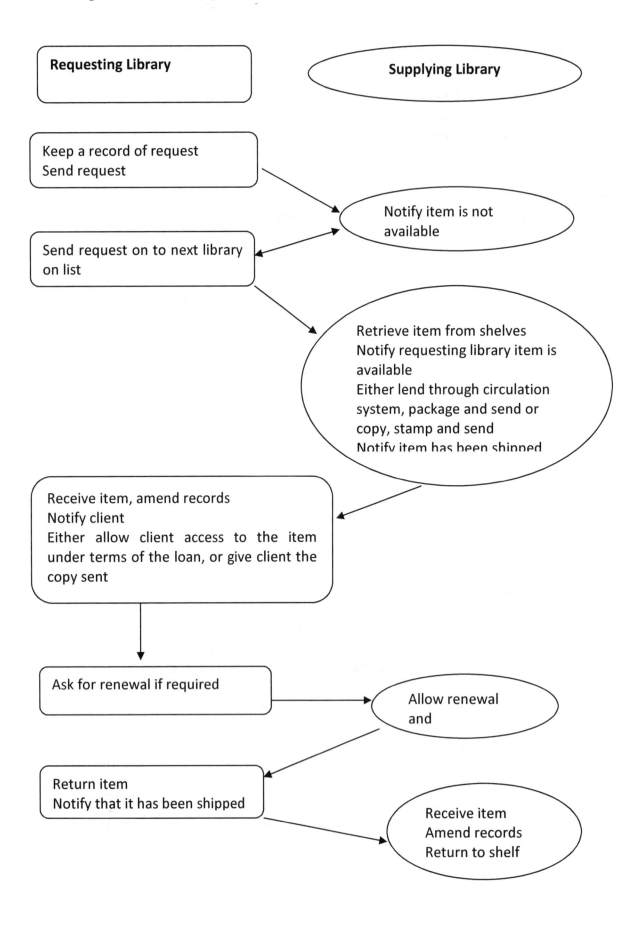

Copyright

If you request a copy rather than the loan of material from another library, you want to be sure that the copy you receive is a legal copy.

When a library copies material, they must comply with the appropriate copyright legislation for their country to ensure they are following the rules on how they can legally copy material.

Libraries are able to copy print material for another library if:
- it is a single copy for a user of the requesting library, or for inclusion in the collection of the requesting library (not a second copy - unless the first copy was lost)

AND
- it is a reasonable portion of a work*

OR
- if not a reasonable portion, the officer in charge of the requesting library must be satisfied that it is not available for purchase in a reasonable time and at a reasonable cost. The officer in charge must sign a statutory declaration to this effect.

*A reasonable portion of a work is not defined for most materials. This depends on the type of material being copied, the reason why it is being copied, and the effect on the market for that item. However for **print** materials, it is considered to be:
- 10% or one chapter (whichever is the greater) of a book of at least ten pages
- one article in a periodical issue
- two or more articles in a periodical issue where they relate to the same subject
- an act of Congress or Parliament, or a court judgment.

It is important to note, however, that requests cannot be filled from a library's licensed electronic resources (i.e. e-journals, e-books, etc.) unless the licenses arranged for those resources include this kind of document supply in their license terms.

This usually means, therefore, that electronic resources cannot be supplied on interlibrary loan if they are available commercially. The portion requested is commercially available when it can be bought on its own (not just as part of a larger resource). So an article in an electronic journal, or one chapter of an e-book cannot be supplied on interlibrary loan if it can be bought at a normal price and supplied in a reasonable time from the commercial supplier.

Copyright Declarations

Whether the request is a reasonable portion or not, the client must sign a statutory declaration to the effect that the copy they have requested is for their personal use or study, and that they have not been supplied with a copy already. It is the responsibility of the requesting library to obtain copyright declarations from their clients for each item to be copied.

The requesting library is required to keep all copyright declarations for the requests they make to other libraries. Copyright Acts do not require libraries to exchange copyright declarations with their requests. Therefore, a supplying library can assume a request received from another library is copyright compliant.

Libraries that participate in interlibrary loan activities must display copyright warnings prominently and they must comply with the copyright law when lending to and borrowing from other libraries. They are required to maintain transaction records for a number of years, as specified in their relevant copyright act.

EXERCISE 6.4 (OPTIONAL)
If you receive ILL requests for these items, decide whether they meet the criteria of the Copyright Act in your country. Which of them require declarations?

1. Kowalski, Suzanne, 'Rhythm, roles and responsibility: the Steiner philosophy explored', *Bedrock*, Vol. 2, issue 4
    and
    Low, Carol and Anh Nguyen, 'Suffer the little children: understanding the needs of child refugees', *Bedrock*, Vol. 2, issue 4

2. The chapter about Ra, the god of radiance (pages 11- 24) in Donna Jo Napoli's book, *Treasury of Egyptian mythology : classic stories of gods, goddesses, monsters & mortals* that was published in Washington, D.C. by National Geographic in 2013. The book has 192 pages.

3. Pages 83-128 of Greenvoe by George Mackay Brown (London, Penguin, 1972) to replace missing pages in the library's copy. It is a 249 page book.

4. The whole of *An outline Of European architecture* by Nikolaus Pevsner. It was published in 1983, has been out of print for 25 years and is rarely seen by secondhand booksellers.

Copying Resources to Send Electronically

Most copyright legislation allows the supplying library to make a digital copy in order to transmit it electronically to the requesting library. The supplying library must destroy the copy after they have transmitted it.

For example, you can scan an article from a print journal and email it. Larger amounts of material may be supplied subject to the commercial availability test previously noted.

Payments

Payment may be made via:

- a central consolidated account if using an ILL network
- by credit card
- by accounts being sent
- by a voucher scheme, such as the one operated by IFLA that is described below.

Payment System for International Interlibrary Transactions

IFLA operates a Voucher Scheme which allows you to pay for your international interlibrary requests, using a voucher instead of money. The scheme is based on a re-useable plastic voucher, which represents a standard payment for one transaction. The Voucher Scheme simplifies payments for international borrowing and document supply. More details about the IFLA Voucher Scheme can be found on the IFLA website at http://www.ifla.org/voucher-scheme.

Best Practice in Interlibrary Loan

'Best practices' are ways to make interlibrary loan services more effective and efficient. To help libraries develop best practices, IFLA has prepared *Guidelines for best practice in interlibrary loan and document delivery* which are described as 'standards for interlibrary loan departments to strive for'. These guidelines are based on several benchmarking studies conducted in North America and Australia. The key findings from these studies determined that best practice is achieved when ILL sections:

- use trained and experienced staff who know their local ILL environment as well as their library's system and procedures
- turn ILL requests around quickly
- reduce the number of hands that handle a request
- automate all processes in the ILL cycle from beginning to end
- establish cooperative agreements with similar libraries.

The IFLA guidelines are on their website at http://www.ifla.org/publications/guidelines-for-best-practice-in-interlibrary-loan-and-document-delivery.

ACTIVITY 6.5
Examine these three documents about resource sharing best practice, or see if your library has a best practice policy for interlibrary loans.

National Resource Sharing Working Group. *Guide to best practice for interlibrary resource sharing in Australia*, 2001.
http://pandora.nla.gov.au/pan/21336/20031011-0000/www.nla.gov.au/initiatives/ilrscode/ilrsbp.html

University of Delaware best practices for interlibrary loan borrowing and lending. Powerpoint prepared by Megan Gaffney, 2009. http://goo.gl/V6Diqh

IFLA. *Guidelines for best practice in interlibrary loan and document delivery.* Last revised 2007. http://www.ifla.org/publications/guidelines-for-best-practice-in-interlibrary-loan-and-document-delivery

Working by yourself or in groups, compare at least two of these documents.

1. Do the documents provide practical suggestions for improving interlibrary loan and document delivery services?

2. Identify one suggestion that you think would help make interlibrary loans in your library (or a library you use) more efficient.

REVISION QUIZ 6.6
Use the following questions to revise your understanding of interlibrary loans. You do not need to write down the answers.

1. Name two ways in which libraries receive ILL requests from other libraries.

2. Name three types of material that libraries prefer not to lend.

3. What methods do libraries use to send items loaned through ILL?

4. Under what circumstances are libraries permitted to copy material for another library?

CHAPTER SEVEN
Acquisitions

Introduction

Libraries acquire materials for the use of their clients in a variety of ways. When a library buys a copy of a book, a music CD, a map and so forth, and stores it, the library is accumulating **assets**. When the library's OPAC points to something on the Internet, for example, and enables clients to retrieve information not stored within the library building, the library is providing **access**.

Since libraries cannot afford to buy all the information sources their clients might want, they combine these two approaches. They buy library materials and store them onsite and they obtain access to information stored elsewhere as requested. This chapter discusses the work performed by acquisitions staff to acquire materials, and the collaborative efforts with public services staff and catalogers to make them available for use by clients.

Assets

Acquisitions work involves buying physical materials such as books and DVDs, receiving them and documenting this in the acquisitions module, then routing the new resources to co-workers for cataloging and physical processing.

Access

Digital text, video and music are available in endless variety; various products, vendors and online platforms market their content and services to libraries. Also referred to as e-resources, they may be ordered in a package that includes many titles or parts, in which case acquisitions staff play a part in keeping track of various types of information, such as:
- which titles or parts are included
- license restrictions on amounts that can be printed or downloaded
- changes to the vendor website
- changes to license fees charged by the vendor.

Acquisitions Functions

The acquisitions department will typically carry out the following functions:
- receive requests for new collection material
- prepare and place orders for new resources
- correspond with, and issue payments to, publishers, distributors, and aggregators
- check materials ordered, ensuring that the library receives what it ordered and what it paid for
- confirm that the online access to e-resources is working
- maintain accurate in-house records of all transactions

- receive and process donations, providing documentation for tax receipts (if eligible for tax deductibility in your country)
- manage exchange agreements with other libraries.

How Libraries Buy Materials for their Collection

Libraries can use various methods to acquire materials (both print/analog and electronic) for their collections:

1. *Firm Orders*

One time purchases through a book vendor service, a bookstore or directly through the publisher. Generally, staff work in collaboration with one or more vendors to acquire materials. Vendors provide libraries with information about a wide variety of titles across subjects of interest to them from different publishers. This allows for a more efficient work flow than if staff had to order materials from individual publishers.

2. *Standing Orders*

An ongoing agreement with a vendor or publisher to supply every issue of a series or a regularly published title. Examples of standing orders are: annual publications such as directories and yearbooks, and research papers that are issued regularly.

3. *Period Orders*

A contract with a vendor for supply of items up to a certain total cost within a specific period, without nominating particular titles at the time of contract. Firm orders can then be placed for individual titles at any time during the contract period. A period order can often include a number of vendors.

4. *Approval Plans*

An ongoing agreement that the vendor or publisher will send every newly published title that meets the criteria outlined in the library's approval profile. Shipments are usually bi-weekly or monthly. The library has the option to review each shipment sent, and accept or promptly send back titles not wanted. Materials may arrive **shelf-ready** with call number labels and barcodes already affixed.

5. *Blanket Orders*

An ongoing agreement to send all titles produced by a particular publisher or supplier. Blanket orders save staff time when a library orders a title each time it is re-issued, such as a directory updated annually. Materials sent through blanket orders are generally not returnable.

6. *Demand-Driven Acquisitions (DDA) for e-Books*

Records for available electronic titles (not yet purchased) are loaded into the catalog to be discovered by library users. When a title is found, clicked on and used (i.e., triggered) the purchase transaction takes place behind the scenes so as to make it appear as though the item was already part of the library's collection. This is also known as patron-driven acquisitions (PDA).

7. Subscription

An annual payment made for a succession of issues over time (subscription period) for a publication that is continuously published, such as a magazine or journal.

8. Lease or License

A regular payment issued for access to online material for a period of time. The terms of the lease or license agreement (how many simultaneous users per title, amount that may be downloaded or printed, etc.) are negotiated with the vendor or publisher.

9. Donation

The library accepts materials as gifts from donors and may issue tax receipts based on a valuation of the material, if tax deductibility is available within the country.

10. Exchange

An arrangement to trade materials with another library based on an agreed profile.

 ACTIVITY 7.1
You can work individually or in a group for this activity.

1. Visit a library acquisitions forum online. One example is Acqweb at www.acqweb.org/. Look around the site to see what services and information are available to acquisitions staff.

2. What are approval plans? Find a description of one on a library book vendor's website.

3. Find an online currency converter and search the prices of a recently published book in your country's currency compared to another currency.

Steps in Acquisition Work

Acquisitions work involves the following:

- receive requests and place orders
- manage blanket orders and approval plans
- receive physical items
- arrange payment
- maintain records of transactions
- liaise with vendors, suppliers, and publishers
- maintain gifts and exchange agreements
- process the material
- process the invoice
- arrange credit notes
- update the order record

Receive Requests and Place Orders

Requests to purchase items can be received in print or in electronic format. A library may create a request form for librarians and other staff to complete and route to the acquisitions department. A copy of an advertisement for, or review of, an item, accompanied by an authorized signature and/or budget code is a common way for requests to be made.

Submission of requests might be continuous throughout the year or requests may come in all at once. For example, college libraries might purchase most of their materials just before a new academic year begins to support the courses that will be taught.

Many web-based catalogs include an online form that registered borrowers can use to send purchase suggestions to the library. It is wise to begin by confirming the library does not already own the item, since a small discrepancy in the title or publication date may cause someone to miss the catalog record. The next step is to verify the bibliographic details, including the price and publisher or supplier, and proceed with ordering.

If the library is using the services of a book vendor with an online system, acquisitions staff will verify bibliographic details and place orders directly onto the vendor's system. Librarians and patrons may be allowed to search the vendor site as well, in which case requests might be flagged or moved into a virtual folder for processing.

Here is a screenshot from a book vendor's website:

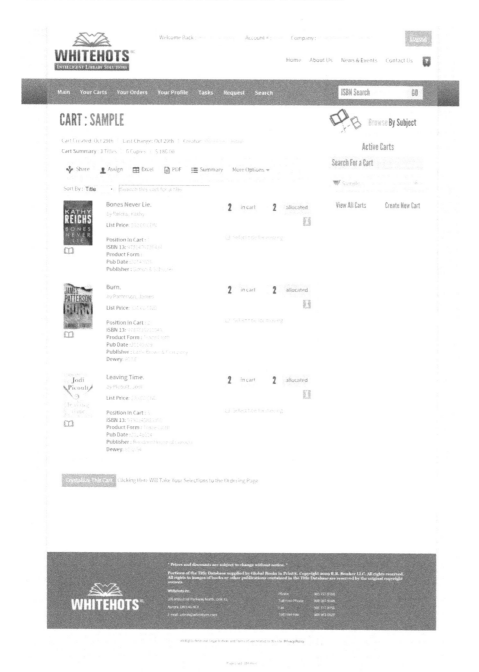

Reprinted with permission of Whitehots, Inc.

Acquisitions staff can manually or electronically request individual resources or groups of resources from specific suppliers. Bibliographic information about the resource (such as title, author, and date of publication), format (such as paperback or e-book), number of copies required, and library order number should be included in the order.

Many libraries divide their budget into several accounts for planning purposes. They use a charge code to indicate which account will be used to pay for the material. Charge codes are also known as account codes or funding codes.

Details of orders, including charge codes if applicable, are recorded in the acquisitions module of the library's management system. In many cases, recording details in the acquisitions module will generate the order and send it to the nominated supplier. Some integrated library systems allow staff to download records from union catalogs, networks or vendor online systems and then use those bibliographic details as order records.

Records from the library's acquisitions module may appear in the OPAC with an 'on order' status. When the resource is received, catalogers update this to a full bibliographic record.

Manage Blanket Orders and Approval Plans

It is quite time-consuming to order individual titles direct from the publisher or bookstore. Blanket orders and approval plans are methods of acquiring materials whereby a supplier, using a library's pre-established collection profile, chooses items in particular categories and disciplines, and ships them to the library on a regular basis. The profile might specify subject area, audience level, format, price range, or language. Blanket orders are usually sent with the understanding that the library will accept everything shipped. Materials shipped via approval plans are subject to inspection and approval and the library can return materials.

Managing these methods of acquisitions involves carefully noting, for each shipment, what the vendor says you have received with what you actually receive and keep.

Receive Physical Items

Receipt of orders includes unpacking boxes, checking documentation, returning errors and defective materials, claiming missing items, and forwarding material for cataloging and processing.

Before Unpacking Boxes:

- Check the address label and confirm (before signing) that the delivery has been sent to the right address.
- Check for enclosed documentation. This is often found under a plastic label on the outside of the box and is marked 'invoice enclosed' or 'packing slip enclosed'. Note that this means that the documentation is enclosed under the outside label, not inside the box.
- Open the box or boxes carefully. Sharp knives may cut through the contents, not just the packaging.

 Occupational Health & Safety Alert
Boxes of books are heavy. Move them carefully and ensure that the weight is evenly distributed on book trucks or they may topple over.

Unpack the box and sort the resources alphabetically, especially if you have a large number of items in the order. This makes checking against the invoice easier. Look inside the box for:
- invoices
- packing slips
- statements
- order reports
- publishers' brochures.

After verifying the address, unpacking the boxes, and locating the documentation:

- Check the items received against the invoice or packing slip.
  Ensure that the items match those included on the documentation and that all items on the invoice or packing slip are actually included.
- Check for damage as you unpack items or as you confirm them against the invoice.
  Physical damage should be referred to a supervisor. In some cases, the decision may be made to accept the item if the damage is minimal or if the item has proved difficult to acquire.
- Check the item received against the on order record.
  Verify that you have the item your library ordered. Pay particular attention to:

    ISBN

    author/title

    edition

    dates of publication

    number of copies

    format (paperback, hardcover, large print, AV).

  Not all differences mean that the item received is unacceptable. A different edition from the one ordered, such as a later edition of a popular work or a differently bound edition, may be acceptable. In these cases, the order record will have to be amended to reflect the actual item received.
- Review the invoice.
  Check the invoiced price against the price quoted on the library purchase order. Usually, the negotiated terms of trade between a supplier and a library, or the library's original order to the supplier, will state an acceptable price variation. If the price variation is greater than agreed upon, the supplier should have notified the library before sending the item, giving the library the opportunity to cancel or confirm the order. Invoices may also need to be checked to ensure that other entitlements such as discounts have been received. The order record should be amended to indicate the actual price paid. This information is useful if additional copies are ordered at a later stage.
- Update the order record
  The order record in an acquisitions module keeps track of what is ordered and received, how much is paid and when. If the public catalog allows patrons to place holds on material on order, when the order status is updated to 'received' the system will inform staff of the Hold. When the item is ready for use, it is routed to circulation rather than to shelving.

The screenshot below shows a firm order record in an acquisitions module, with brief bibliographic information (author, title, call number) displayed above the order record:

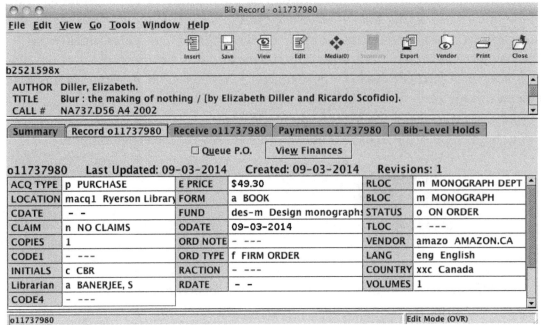

Software copyright Innovative Interfaces, Inc. Used with permission

Arrange Payment

In large institutions, this might involve sending the necessary documentation authorizing payment to an Accounts Payable department. In small operations, you might mail a check or authorize an account debit. Once money in an account or fund has been set aside to pay for items the library has received, the amount is said to be **encumbered**.

In the acquisitions module of an ILS (integrated library system), the order record is updated by adding a received date or by changing the status from 'On order' to 'Received'. Then the invoice (the document that requests payment from the library) is processed.

The invoice lists the items supplied and their cost. The library's order number for each individual item should be quoted on the invoice.

The invoice may also include information about the terms of payment. The total cost invoiced may differ from the sum of the individual items if there are additional line items such as discounts or freight charges.

Invoices may be sent separately from the materials themselves, especially in the case of overseas items. They are usually sent airmail in advance of the parcel. This allows the library to know what is due and makes it easier to follow up on items that are not received.

Most ILS acquisitions modules and vendors use **Electronic Data Interchange (EDI)** to exchange information such as invoices, purchase orders, claims, and other business documents.

Some libraries participate in consortium purchases for collections or online services. This allows libraries to pool their efforts and lease or buy resources as a group, and share the financial cost and administrative staff time of managing the electronic resources. The libraries in such a collaborative arrangement may be grouped by geography (for example, all libraries in a state or province) or by type of library (for example, all academic libraries in a region).

Maintain Records of Transactions

Libraries are accountable for the funds they receive. Therefore, staff must keep accurate records of all transactions to document how the money is spent. The acquisitions module in the ILS may be able to run reports that can be exported.

Acquisitions staff may assist with the preparation of budget statements and with the allocation of the acquisitions budget among the various funds or accounts. For these reasons, bookkeeping and accounting skills are important in this type of work.

Liaise with Vendors, Suppliers, and Publishers

Acquisitions staff provide the link between the library and the various agencies with which it does business. Libraries might purchase items from trade publishers who sell materials that appeal to a wide general audience. Often, however, they prefer to deal with wholesalers who handle trade books from various publishers to save the time of negotiating and corresponding with many individual publishers. Academic and special libraries may need to buy materials directly from publishers who produce books in specific fields or disciplines. Medical, legal, and scientific and technical publishers, university presses, private presses, and government departments supply items that trade publishers do not carry because the market for this information is small and sales are limited.

Maintain Gifts and Exchange Agreements

Some libraries accept donations of books and other materials to add to their collections. Most donations are unsolicited and are offered to a library when someone moves or empties out their office. Donated materials often need to be evaluated because donors may expect a tax receipt in countries where they are able to claim tax deductions.

Libraries set up arrangements to exchange materials with each other. Usually, a group of libraries will agree to produce and exchange lists of unwanted and duplicate materials (such as issues of serials) on a regular basis. The first library to request an item on the list receives the item and pays to have it shipped.

Gifts and exchanges save the cost of purchasing this information. They still require an investment of staff time to receive the items, to determine if they are suitable for the collection, and then to catalog and process them for circulation to library users. These materials may be recorded in the acquisitions files in the same way as ordered items but without the financial information. 'Gift' or 'exchange' may replace the supplier information.

EXERCISE 7.2

These four books and their invoice arrived in today's delivery. You have searched the books in the acquisitions module and found their order records, included below. Do all the necessary checks to identify any problems with the delivery.

J. R. R. TOLKIEN

THE HOBBIT
or
THERE AND BACK AGAIN

Douglas & McIntyre   2013

edited by
Richard Aitken
and Michael Looker

Oxford University Press
South Melbourne
2002

ISBN 9780195536447

East Coast Library Services

INVOICE NO: 1413396   **DATE:**   2014/04/03
TO Northside Library & Archives, 23 Main Street

ORDER #	AUTHOR /TITLE	Units	ISBN	PRICE
3679	The oil man and the sea: navigating the northern gateway	1	9781771001076	24.95
3217	Sport as a business	1	9780230249257	54.72
3643	The hobbit, or, There and back again	1	9780261103283	21.75
3228	The Oxford companion to Australian gardens	1	9780195536447	95.13
	Subtotal			226.55
	Delivery & ST			13.98
	TOTAL			**$250.53**

Order records in the acquisitions module of the ILS:

File Edit View Insert Format Tools Window Help

Order number	**3217**	Account/ fund	**Mono - bus**
Date ordered	**2014-02-03**	Date received	---
No. of copies	**1**	Status	**o – on order**
Title	**Sport as a business international, professional and commercial aspects**	Order type	**f- firm order**
Author/ editor	**Dolles**	Form	**n – ebook**
Edition		Librarian	**js**
Vendor	**y - YBP**		
Notes	**ISBN: 9780230249257 On Hold for p338002**		

File Edit View Insert Format Tools Window Help

Order number	**3643**	Account/ fund	**Mono - lit**
Date ordered	**2014-02-11**	Date received	---
No. of copies	**1**	Status	**o – on order**
Title	**The hobbit or there and back again**	Order type	**f- firm order**
Author/ editor	**Tolkien**	Form	**p – print book**
Edition	**70th Anniversary**	Librarian	**sb**
Vendor	**y - YBP**		
Notes	**ISBN: 9780261103283**		

File Edit View Insert Format Tools Window Help

Order number	**3228**	Account/ fund	**Mono - des**
Date ordered	**2014-01-30**	Date received	---
No. of copies	**1**	Status	**o – on order**
Title	**Australian gardens**	Order type	**f- firm order**
Author/ editor	**Aitkens**	Form	**p – print book**
Edition	**Oxford companions**	Librarian	**ne**
Vendor	**y - YBP**		
Notes	**ISBN 9780195536447**		

<u>F</u>ile <u>E</u>dit <u>V</u>iew <u>I</u>nsert For<u>m</u>at <u>T</u>ools <u>W</u>indow <u>H</u>elp

Order number	**3679**	Account/ fund	**Mono - gen**
Date ordered	**2014-02-20**	Date received	**---**
No. of copies	**1**	Status	**o – on order**
Title	**The oil man and the sea navigating the northern gateway**	Order type	**f- firm order**
Author/ editor	**Kopecky**	Form	**n – ebook**
Edition		Librarian	**js**
Vendor	**y - YBP**		
Notes			

1. Are there any differences between the resources received, the invoice and the order records?
   The oil man and the sea

   The Hobbit

   Sport as a business

   Australian gardens

2. Did you notice any notes on the order records that require further attention?

3. Are there any errors in the order records?

Process the Material

Processing involves physical preparation of the item received, and paperwork for the invoice and the order record. Acquisitions processing varies from library to library, but there are common principles. It is very important to follow the library's procedures exactly.

Acquisitions processing may include:

- adding a stamp to show ownership - this is done immediately
- recording the order number, price and/or accession number on the item (often in pencil, on the title page or verso depending on library policy). What is recorded will vary for different formats, particularly non-book material
- attaching a barcode
- inserting an instruction slip if there are special procedures to be followed, such as the material is for specific collections (for example, reference), it is to be referred to a particular client on receipt, or processed urgently because there is a Hold. These instructions would be noted in the order record.

The newly received item should be kept if:

- there are no problems with the item
- it was not the ordered item but a decision has been made to accept it instead of the ordered item
- it was not the ordered item but a decision has been made to accept it as well as the ordered item. In this case, a confirming order is drawn up.

If the item is to be returned, **it must not be marked**.

Process the Invoice

If an item is to be kept:

- sign and date the invoice, to acknowledge responsibility for the order and to authorize payment
- record the charge code on the invoice, to indicate from which part of the budget funds are to be drawn
- if a new confirming order has been drawn up, change the order number on the invoice to the new order number.

If the item is to be returned:

- mark the item 'to be returned' on the invoice and
- depending on library policy, either deduct the amount not to be paid from the invoice total or note the number of the credit note (if any) on the invoice
- send the invoice to the accounts section.

Arrange Credit Notes

Material to be returned requires a credit note to reduce the total of the invoice before payment. Credit notes are documents authorizing a difference between the invoiced cost and the actual price paid. Credit notes cannot be used to lower the price of an item you are keeping, unless you have prior approval from the supplier.

There are several procedures for arranging a credit on an invoice:

- The library may request a corrected invoice, and delay passing the invoice for payment. This is the practice for suppliers with which the library deals infrequently.
- The supplier is asked for a credit note, and the invoice is paid only after it is received. This is an alternative for suppliers with which the library deals infrequently.
- The invoice is paid and the supplier is asked for a credit note, which is used to reduce a future invoice. This is one practice for suppliers with which the library deals frequently.
- Major library suppliers allow their regular customer libraries to issue a credit note on stationery which they supply. The item is returned to the supplier with a copy of the credit note, and the credit note number is recorded on the invoice. The invoice is passed to the account section with a copy of the credit note, indicating which items are not to be paid.

 Here is an example of a credit note:

ALWAYS LIBRARY SUPPLIERS
CREDIT NOTE NO: 2034

FROM   Southern Institute Library
Could St
Canberra ACT

Invoice no	Order no	Title	Invoice cost	Reason for return
b4738	9500245	Exit lines	$13.95	copy misbound
b4738	9500758	In the frame	$39.96	paperback ordered, hardcover supplied

Update the Order Record

If an item is to be kept, the order record in the acquisitions module of the ILS is updated:

- Enter the date of receipt.
- Note the correct price.
- Update any bibliographic information that has changed (especially where you have accepted an item instead of another) or flag it for the cataloger.
- Add the invoice number, accession number and/or bank check number.
- Entering the received date usually results in the order record status changing from 'on order' to 'in-process' by the system. Otherwise you may be required to change the status field to 'received' or something similar.
- The invoice is ready to send to the accounts section for payment.

Here is a sample acquisitions work flow.

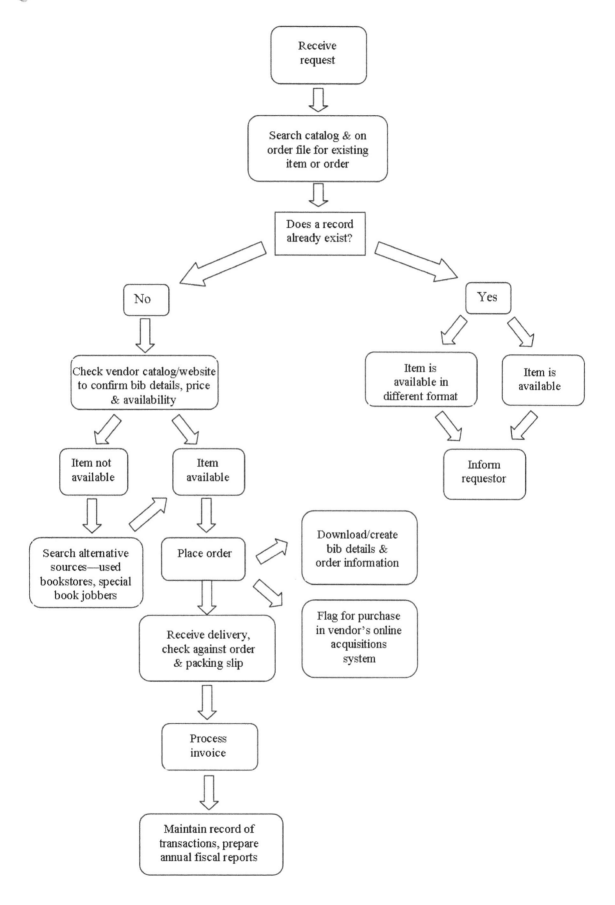

Items With Problems

Once problems are identified, a decision must be made whether to accept the item despite the problem. This is made in consultation with a supervisor and perhaps the selection staff. You may even consult the library client who requested the item.

Items are returned only if they are unusable. Consider the immediate need for the book and the cost, as well as the time and inconvenience of returning it and waiting for a new copy.

On some occasions where the book is wanted urgently but arrives damaged, you may use the damaged copy and demand a replacement or a credit on the purchase price.

Items cannot be returned just because you have changed your mind.

Problem	Action
Minor damage	Can possibly be fixed or ignored. Consider the condition of a book after a few uses. Consider how urgently you need the information.
Major damage – e.g., water, pages missing, misbound	If the book is unusable, return it awaiting a replacement copy or keep the damaged copy until the replacement is received.
Wrong edition	Earlier editions are almost always unwanted. This often occurs when new editions are ordered from prepublishing information. Later editions are normally acceptable, but there are situations when it will not be (e.g., when the library wants to buy a particular edition as a replacement copy for a missing item).
Wrong ISBN	Look further before you accept or reject the item. Different ISBNs don't mean different items. It means you should check the other bibliographic information carefully. Different casings (hardback/paperback) and editions published in different places probably have the same contents, and may or may not be acceptable as alternatives in your library. Price, likely usage and strength of the binding may influence the choice. Possibly the only problem may have been the typing in your orders section. ISBNs are difficult to type correctly every time.
Partial order arrives (too few copies or fewer parts than ordered)	Accept this and await rest of order. Unless there is a notice in your order reports, contact the supplier to ensure they are still aware that they have not completed the order. Depending on your library policy and your arrangements with the vendor, you may be able to make a partial payment against the invoice.

Items not on invoice	Check you haven't missed a second invoice in the packaging.
	The item could still be intended for you, but was left off the invoice—check your order records. Contact the supplier if so.
	The item may have strayed into your delivery and be intended for another library. Return it.
On invoice but not in your order records	Check the orders-complete file, in case the supplier is filling an order already received or previously cancelled.
	Consider other order records in your library. Could it be part of a standing order or a blanket order? Could it have been sent as a standing order where you only intended a single monograph order? The order number on the invoice may give you a clue.
	Bibliographic information could have changed after you ordered the item. Check by order number.
Wrong item sent	May send it back and await the correct item.
	May want to keep this as well as receiving the original.
	May accept it instead of the ordered title.
Incorrect price	Normally the library will have limits to the price variations it will accept, and the supplier should be aware of these. Any variations in price greater than these should be checked with the library before supply.
	Prices vary with exchange fluctuations, and with normal price increases. Some prices on your orders are very old, some are estimates when the orders staff were unable to find a price.
	Some items you will want no matter what they cost; some you will only want if they are within your range.
	You may query the cost of an item or send it back and cancel your order, but only if the price is substantially different.

At the end of this process you will have material in five different categories:
1. material as ordered ready to be processed
2. material you will accept instead of the ordered material
3. material you want to keep as well as receiving the material ordered
4. material about which you need more information from the supplier
5. material you want to return.

1. Material as Ordered Ready to be Processed
Process it as described below. Pass it to the cataloging section for cataloging and final processing.

2. Accept Instead of the Ordered Material
Alter the order record to conform to the item received, and process it as though the correct item was received.

3. Keep in Addition to the Material Ordered
If there is material you want to keep as well as acquiring the material you ordered, you will have to draw up a **confirming order**. A new order record with a new order number is created, clearly marked 'confirming order - item received', so that a second copy of the item is not sent. The original request is left on order, and all processing is done using the new order. Contact the supplier to notify them that you still expect the original order. Update any bibliographic information that has changed (especially if you have accepted an item that is different from what was ordered) or flag it for the cataloger.

4. You Need More Information from the Supplier
Sometimes it is difficult to make a decision without more information. In these cases, hold the item without processing while the information is gathered. This is often done when a price is incorrect and you think it may be the supplier's error.

Email, fax, phone or send a form letter to the supplier stating the order number, title, invoice number and summary of the problem. Make the decision to keep or return the item when the reply comes.

Often the invoice is held pending a reply. If the reply takes some time, sometimes a credit note can be used, to allow the rest of the invoice to be paid. The item is re-invoiced when a solution is found.

5. Material You Want to Return
If an item is to be returned, **it must not be marked**. Once the copy is stamped or written in, it will have to be paid for.

ACTIVITY 7.3
Two of the items in Exercise 7.2 were not as ordered. Discuss with other students or colleagues whether a library is likely to want these items or not, and which of the above categories applies:

Serial Publication Control

The term **serial** refers to a publication issued in separate parts. The parts, or issues, are numbered (e.g., vol. 10, no. 3) or have chronological designations (e.g., January 2014). A serial is intended to be published indefinitely, meaning there is no end date of publication in mind when the first issue is published. They are generally issued regularly (monthly, bimonthly, etc.), although this is not mandatory. Serials may be created in any medium: print, electronic, microform, and so forth.

Careful control of incoming issues of serials enables a library to get maximum value for its subscription dues. Serial control systems vary, but most can answer the following questions:
- What is the latest issue received?
- Are any issues missing or unavailable for some other reason?
- How often does the library send issues for binding?
- Where can one subscribe to the publication?
- When is the library's subscription due for renewal?

Because serials are published over a period of time, they often undergo many changes. A serial might:
- cease publication permanently or temporarily
- change titles
- merge with another title to become a new serial
- change size or format
- split into two separate titles
- publish special issues or supplements, sometimes with separate titles
- change publishers or subject matter
- change frequency.

Maintain Access to Electronic Serial Collections

Many serials are also published electronically and made available online. They are called e-journals and are often packaged together by publisher or subject and sold to libraries by **aggregators.** It is possible to subscribe individually to e-journal titles but most libraries use aggregator services for bulk acquisition of electronic journals.

Aggregators are agencies that acquire the distribution rights for different pieces of information and then offer the pieces as a package. Aggregators sell libraries web-based full-text databases that include journals, magazines, and newspapers in electronic format. These journals, magazines, and newspapers are often all published separately. The aggregator negotiates licenses with the publishers and then distributes the information with 'added value' services such as a search engine and the option to send documents to an email address.

Electronic serials are often more complex to manage because they are not shipped to the library as are print materials, but are accessed over networks. User names, passwords, and Internet addresses are features of electronic serials subscriptions that the print versions do not require.

Acquisitions staff may assist with the setting up of test accounts for an electronic package to be evaluated by librarians and library users such as faculty. They might also coordinate the signing of license agreements and communicate with systems staff regarding passwords and links from the online catalog.

Electronic Resources Management (ERM) is a concept designed to assist libraries with the control of information needed to acquire and provide access to licensed electronic resources such as databases and online portals containing electronic books, journals, videos and music. Ensuring that payments are made, licenses are signed and filed, and URLs that point to the digital resources actually work is referred to as electronic resource management.

ERM work can include managing email messages from librarians and vendors, maintaining spreadsheets of information about products, filing and archiving license agreements and documents with site URLs and administrative passwords.

ERM software might be stand-alone or included as a module within the library's integrated library system. ERM software helps staff to:

- describe payments and other financial and subscription details that are unique to digital resources and to link these details to bibliographic records
- prepare specific records to keep track of licensing details, URLs, usernames and passwords, IP addresses, and contact information
- provide a customized OPAC display of information useful to users, such as printing permissions and interlibrary loan availability.

Because electronic journals are automatically available from the start of the subscription, there are no check-in, handling, claiming or routing processes needed. These processes, however, are important in the control of print journals.

Control of Print Serial Titles

In this section we focus on receiving print subscriptions and maintaining their check-in records. The procedure for receiving serial issues is the same for manual and automated systems. **Check-in record** refers to either a manual or an automated file. The serials control steps include:

1. Check the address label to ensure that issues have arrived at the correct destination.
2. Open and inspect for damage; check for accompanying information; retain packaging.
3. Sort into priority order.
4. Locate the check-in record.
5. Record receipt carefully and accurately.
6. Stamp the issue and process by adding call numbers, barcodes, and so on, according to library policy.
7. Notify cataloging staff if any information has changed (e.g., title change, ceased publication, new supplement included).
8. Attach routing slips for circulated titles.
9. Claim late issues.

1. Check the address label to ensure that issues have arrived at the correct destination
For example, in large organizations, other departments may have their own subscriptions to serial titles or newspapers that are also ordered for the library.

2. Open and inspect for damage; check for accompanying information; retain packaging
Items in poor condition and not suitable for client use should be replaced. However, a substitute copy may not always be available and is usually requested only in cases where there is substantial damage.

Accompanying material may be:
- renewal invoices
- notices of change of title
- notice of ceasing or suspended publication
- advertising material
- notices of conferences.

Renewal notices should be routed to the appropriate person for processing. Change of title and/or publication information requires amendment of the check-in record. Advertising material is given to selection staff. Notices of conferences may be kept with the issue, displayed separately, or sent to clients according to their interests.

The packaging should be kept with the issue in case it includes details the person updating the check-in record will need. The packaging may also provide reference numbers that can be used to trace orders.

3. Sort into priority order
If many titles are being received, the serials may be sorted alphabetically by title, by date of receipt, or in priority order for processing. Titles received by airmail, as well as daily and weekly publications, are usually processed as a priority.

4. Locate the check-in record
Locate the record for the title in hand by searching the library's file of check-in records. Check-in records are generally searched by title, ISSN, or SICI (Serial Item and Contribution Identifier)—a barcode attached by the publisher to make serials check-in more efficient. Libraries with automated serials systems can scan the SICI barcode and the system then records the issue as received.

Check carefully that the title in hand matches the serial check-in record. Libraries may receive several serials with similar titles or there may be a title change or merger.

Verify that the expected issue has arrived, whether an issue has been missed, or whether the one in hand is actually a duplicate copy. Look for the issue information on front cover, the title page, or the spine. The information may be:
- a chronological designation (e.g., 5/5/14 or 5 May 2014 or Fall 2014)
- a volume and number designation (e.g., Vol. 16, no. 4)
- a number (e.g., No. 1345)
- a combination of the above.

5. Record receipt carefully and accurately

Attention to detail is essential, and the work often calls for some problem-solving. It is important to record the exact issues and date of receipt.

Consistent and accurate data entry provides staff and library users with comprehensive holdings information and saves the time and effort often spent looking for 'missing' issues.

If the library's ILS has a serials check-in module, it will assist staff to keep track of the details of newly received serials. Check-in records in an ILS may include the following report functions:

- which titles are currently being received
- which issues of inactive titles are held
- which titles are on order or in process
- when issues of each title are received and an estimate of when the next issue is due
- processing information such as location, call number, holdings policy, binding information
- special instructions for cataloging serial issues individually
- supply problems such as missing issues, lapsed subscriptions, and the action taken
- order and renewal information (e.g., supplier, order number)
- a history of payments.

Most online systems can be set up to print routing slips and claim forms.

This is the check-in record for a journal from an ILS. The record tracks details such as frequency of publication, whether the title is currently received (or not), and the vendor.

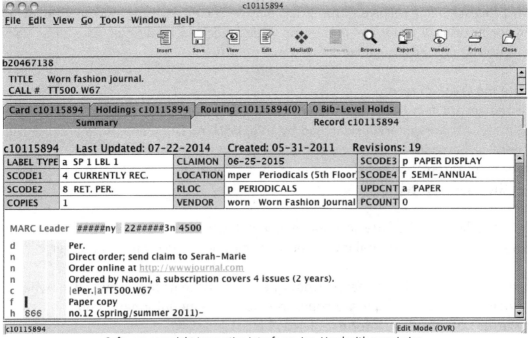

Software copyright Innovative Interfaces, Inc. Used with permission

This is the check-in card tracking which issues have been received and which are expected.

Software copyright Innovative Interfaces, Inc. Used with permission

6. Stamp the issue and process

Stamp the issue with the library's ownership stamp, which often includes the date received.

Mark the issue with the call number, taking care that labels do not cover important information, such as the title, volume number, or date.

Attach barcodes, date due labels, security strips, and so on, according to library policy.

7. Notify cataloging staff if any information has changed

If it appears that a title has changed, has ceased publication, or has arrived with a new supplement, route to the cataloging department. Catalog records for serials can be updated to include notes explaining variant titles, accompanying supplements, and publishing information.

8. Attach routing slips for circulated titles

Journal circulation or routing means sending new serial issues to selected library clients. Serials staff might circulate a list of all the titles the library is willing to circulate and ask users to indicate what they wish to see. This service is often offered by special libraries to their users and by academic or school libraries to staff. Such a service is good public relations.

Journal circulation puts the information in people's hands and allows them to read it when it arrives, without having to monitor the library's new issues shelves. Clients like the service and it makes them aware of the library.

When an issue arrives and is checked in, a prepared list of clients is attached to the issue that is then routed to the first person on the list. Occasionally you may need to add or remove names from the list.

The disadvantage of routing is that it may be impossible to know exactly where an issue is, or when it will return. The library is therefore required to encourage people to read and pass on the issues, in a timely manner, to the next person on the routing list.

9. Claim late issues

Serials are complex, and their ongoing maintenance and control is labor-intensive. For this reason, many libraries employ subscription agents to help them manage serial subscriptions. If the library does not have a subscription agent, claims are sent directly to the publisher or distributor.

Late issues are common, and serials are known to be unpredictable. After a number of weeks or months, the library might send a claim notice to inquire about the status of a title (e.g., Has it ceased or been suspended?) The claim notice might be a form letter, either typed by hand or generated from the online system. Keep in mind that claiming too quickly after the expected date might result in duplicate issues.

Some received and circulated issues might not be in any condition to go for binding when the time comes. It is sometimes necessary to re-order missing and damaged issues from either the subscription agent or the publisher, often at a higher price.

EXERCISE 7.4

Search OCLC WorldCat or another catalog to answer the following questions about serials:

1. What is the full title of a serial called *Women & literature*? What is the ISSN?

2. What is the title of the serial with ISSN 0949-149X? Is it still being published?

3. When was the first issue of *Chemical abstracts* published?

4. *The journal of supply change management* (published by the National Association of Purchasing Management) has changed its title several times. Give one of its former titles with ISSN.

5. *Rolling Stone* is American but is there also an Australian edition? If so, do any American libraries have a subscription to it?

CHAPTER EIGHT
Collection Maintenance

Introduction
The work of maintaining library collections includes ensuring the materials stay usable over time. This is done by preparing materials for circulation, monitoring signs of use and damage, following established storage and shelving practices, and, in some cases, disposing of, or replacing items.

What Is Collection Maintenance?
Collection maintenance involves the following tasks:
- **Final processing**: (also known as end processing or physical processing), the physical preparation of library materials for shelving and patron use. This may involve covering or strengthening materials that will be loaned.
- **Storage**: different materials require different storage methods since they can vary greatly in kind, size, and shape (e.g., atlases, maps, books, pamphlets, DVDs).
- **Shelving**: placing new materials on the shelves or replacing items after use.
- **Care of the collection**: providing the correct environment for the materials, checking their physical condition, and repairing damaged materials.
- **Inventory and shelf reading**: reading call numbers to ensure materials are on the shelf and in the correct order.

Collection maintenance is important because:
- library materials are often expensive and may be impossible to replace
- materials should be kept in good condition and correct order to make sure that they are accessible and ready to use
- patrons are more inclined to use materials that are in good condition and tend to avoid shabby or damaged materials.

Processing
Usually items are cataloged and classified before they are sent for physical processing to make them ready for use. Processing is typically divided into two stages:
- materials receipt
- final processing.

1. Materials Receipt
There are processing tasks that are carried out when the item is first received and before it is cataloged and classified. These tasks include:

Checking
When an item is received, it must be checked carefully to make sure that it is the item requested and that it is in good physical order. For example, ensure that a book has all of its pages or a kit has all of its parts.

Ownership Marks
Ownership marks are used to show that the item is the property of the library. In the case of books, this mark is usually an ink stamp put in a number of places—usually on the verso of the title page and on other designated pages throughout the book. If an item is rare or valuable, ownership marks are not used on the item itself.

Accessioning
Historically, libraries assigned each item a unique identifying number called an accession number. This was usually a running number, written on each item and in a register to record how many items were acquired since the collection began. Record numbers in ILS systems or barcodes are now commonly used instead of accession numbers in libraries. Most archives and some special collections continue to assign accession numbers.

Materials receipt is part of the acquisitions process and chapter 7 of this workbook goes into more detail about all aspects, including administrative tasks, of this process.

2. Final Processing
The tasks that are completed after the item has been cataloged and classified include:

Call Number Labels
An adhesive label with the call number, usually generated from the cataloging module of the ILS, is affixed to the spine or front cover.

The call number determines the item's location on the shelf and gives patrons an exact 'address' to find materials they need. It may include the physical location such as a branch library or a special collection (e.g., the reference collection). It may also provide a copy number (e.g., Copy 2).

Special Symbols
- **Locations**: some items are sent to branch libraries or special collections and need specific identification. Often color codes are used to indicate different locations if this information is not included in the call number.
- **Type of material**: location symbols are also used for various categories of materials such as serials and audiovisual items.
- **Circulation information**: symbols may be used to indicate circulation information. For example, a red dot may indicate that an item cannot be borrowed.

Security
Magnetic security strips (also referred to as tattle tape) or Radio-frequency Identification (RFID) tags may be inserted as part of a library's security system.

Magnetic strips set off an alarm when they are passed through security gates. They are meant to be desensitized at the time of borrowing and resensitized on their return.

Radio-frequency Identification (RFID) tags produce a low-level radio frequency that is detected by a reader. RFID readers can scan multiple items with tags at once and relay the information to the ILS circulation module. Materials with RFID tags can be circulated, returned and sorted very efficiently.

Covering
A plastic jacket or adhesive cover strengthens a book and protects against soiling. With the exception of adhesive covering, the covering should be attached in such a way that it can be removed for re-covering in future.

Strengthening Strips
Vinyl tape or adhesive covering strips may be used to strengthen weak book bindings. Corners may also be strengthened in this way.

Final Check
The item must be checked to make sure that all of the processing stages have been completed before it can be shelved ready for patron use.

Remember to:
- *use the materials as economically as possible*
- *handle the items with care*
- *keep your work area tidy.*

ACTIVITY 8.1

Visit a library and examine an example of each format listed below. Look at the method used to process the item and fill in the table.

	Printed book	Serial	Map	Video on DVD
Where is the library's ownership stamp?				
Can you find a barcode on the item?				
Where is the call number on the item?				
Does the item have a special cover or packaging?				
Are there any special symbols on the item such as a sticker to indicate reference?				

EXERCISE 8.2

Libraries purchase the materials needed to maintain and preserve their collections from library suppliers. Using a library supplier's online or print catalog, look at the products that can be used to process library materials. Compare two different formats (e.g., DVDs and maps) and fill in the table.

	Maps	DVDs
What products are available in the catalog?		
How much do the products cost?		
Do the products vary from those you saw in the library?		
Suggest reasons the library chose its methods.		

ACTIVITY 8.3

Compare the following steps for processing a new book with the process followed by a library nearby, or with a manual you can find online (many university libraries post some documentation online):

1. Apply the ownership stamp as per library policy. Possible locations:
   the verso of the title page
   on a page approximately halfway through the item, in the margin and not obscuring text or images
   the inside of the back cover.

2. Apply a barcode or RFID tag in the appropriate place.

3. Write the call number in pencil within the ownership stamp on the verso of the title page.

4. Apply tattle tape
   hardback: place one-sided tattle tape down the spine
   paperback: place double-sided tattle tape between two pages.

5. Create a call number label: for example
   023.0994
        CAT

6. Apply the call number label on the spine if the book is 1.5 cm wide or thicker, positioning it 1.5 cm. from the base of the spine. For narrower items, place label on lower front cover, 1 cm. from the bottom edge and 1 cm. from the spine.

7. Apply a location symbol above the call number label if required.

8. Check that all stages have been completed and ask an experienced staff member to review your work.

Storage of Library Materials
Introduction
Libraries collect a range of materials that vary in kind, size, and shape as well as ones that may require special storage.

Choosing the correct form of storage for each format is important in order to ensure that all items remain in good condition.

The storage method chosen for particular materials depends on the following factors:
- cost
- appearance
- the space available
- the library's clientele
- the need to prevent damage to materials
- staffing levels
- the rarity of the materials
- the particular needs of specific formats.

Different Formats
Most libraries have separate sequences of shelving to house different sizes and formats of materials. They generally use adjustable shelving to cater for these different requirements. If different types of materials are shelved together, the library has to allow the maximum height on each shelf. This takes up a lot of extra space.

Printed Books
Most books are stored on bookshelves with book supports to keep them upright. They should not be shelved too tightly because they are likely to be damaged when users try to remove them. Although books can withstand frequent handling before needing repair or rebinding, some libraries cover books to prolong their life. Paperback books may be stored in wire bookracks for ease of access. Large books should be stored horizontally on shelves, but if several are piled on top of each other, the weight causes damage.

Manuscripts
Rare or valuable manuscripts may need to be stored in a secure area such as a locked storeroom or cupboard. If they are on flat sheets, manuscripts may be bound into books, filed in loose-leaf folders, or stored in boxes. Rolled manuscripts are stored in cylinders.

Pamphlets
These are usually stored in pamphlet boxes on shelves. Some libraries store them in filing cabinets or place them in stiff covers and shelve them upright with the main collection of books.

Pamphlet boxes protect the materials, and users find them easy to handle, but the thickness of the boxes takes up extra space on the shelves. A filing cabinet for pamphlets protects them from light and dust, but the cabinet takes up floor space.

Periodicals

Most libraries display current issues of periodicals on racks that hold the items rigid. Some use transparent plastic covers to protect the issues. Back runs of periodicals may be bound and shelved in the same way as books. Unbound back issues of periodicals are usually stored in pamphlet boxes.

Maps, Plans, and Diagrams

These formats are best stored flat in plan cabinets, but some libraries roll and store them in plastic, metal, or cardboard cylinders placed in pigeon-hole racks. If they are fragile, they should be interleaved with acid-free paper. Frequently used items may be laminated.

Pictures

Drawings and photographs may be stored in folders in a filing cabinet or mounted in albums. Another option is to use archival boxes that protect the items from light and dust.

Newspapers

Recent issues of newspapers are often stored in a hanging file. Older issues may be bound and stored horizontally on specially designed shelving. Some libraries store older issues in archive boxes or shrink-wrap their newspapers. Because newsprint deteriorates quickly, many libraries preserve the information by digitizing the issues and making them available electronically.

Microforms

Microfiche may be stored in envelopes, boxes, or slotted plastic panels. Microfilm is usually stored in small reels in cardboard boxes that are housed in cabinets.

Films and Slides

Roll film is best stored in metal canisters. Filmstrips may be stored in boxes. Slides are usually housed in slotted drawers or in transparent plastic sleeves.

Sound Recordings and DVDs

CDs and DVDs may be stored on display racks, in a tower, or on shelves.

ACTIVITY 8.4
Visit a library and identify as many formats of material as possible using the list in the table below. Take note of how the materials are stored and fill in the details.

Type of Material	Held in Library?	Storage Methods
Printed books		
Pamphlets		
Periodicals		
Maps, plans, diagrams		
Photographs		
Newspapers		
CDs and DVDs		

EXERCISE 8.5

Examine a library supplier's catalog and identify the types of equipment and materials available for storing the library materials listed in Activity 8.2.

*Choose **two** formats of library materials - one print and one non-print - and compare the way in which they are stored in a library with the methods of storage shown in the supplier's catalog. Take into consideration the reasons the library chose its method of storage. State which method you think is the most effective.*

	Print Format	**Non-Print Format**
Material		
Storage method used in library		
One storage method suggested in supplier's catalog		
Reasons library chose its method		
Effectiveness of chosen method		

EXERCISE 8.6

Based on your observations in a library, describe three examples of storage methods that may cause problems for library materials and for users. Suggest solutions to these problems.

	Example 1	**Example 2**	**Example 3**
Methods that cause problems for materials			
Possible solutions to problems			
Methods that cause problems for users			
Possible solutions to problems			

REVISION QUIZ 8.7

Use the following questions to revise your understanding of collection maintenance. You do not need to write down the answers.

1. Why is it important to maintain the physical objects in a collection?

2. What is a spine label?

3. Why do libraries cover books?

4. What is meant by final processing?

5. Name three factors that will affect the storage methods chosen by a library.

CHAPTER NINE
Shelving of Physical Resources

Introduction

The ideal situation in a library is to shelve all of the physical resources on a particular topic together, in order to make maximum use of all materials. In many libraries, however, the varied formats of library materials, the need for security, a shortage of shelf space and the costs involved in processing materials lead to the physical segregation of different types of material.

The physical segregation of material may alter usage patterns and the demand for materials. Each library needs to consider its own circumstances and user needs. There is no arrangement that can be applied universally.

Different Shelving Arrangements
Access
Closed Access

Also known as closed stacks, these are storage areas not accessible by the public. This arrangement does not allow the library user to collect materials directly from the shelves, so staff must be available to do this. Sometimes collections in this area are housed in accession number order rather than arranged by subject, so as to save space and for easier retrieval.

Open Access

With this arrangement users can browse and retrieve materials from the shelves. Most libraries are open access and arranged by subject to make browsing possible.

Factors to Consider in Making the Choice Between Closed And Open Access

When deciding whether to make the collection open or closed access, libraries base their decision on a number of factors, including:

- the nature of the collection (whether the material is up-to-date or archival)
- the size of the collection and the accommodation available
- the need to avoid damage caused by handling
- the availability of staff to service the collection
- the cost and difficulty of replacing items
- the availability and location of equipment necessary to use an item
- the need to preserve the privacy of the material.

It is common for parts of a collection to be closed access, while other sections are open access. Closed access areas may include non-print materials, reserve and high demand collections, archives, manuscripts and rare books.

Location

Fixed Location

This system is mainly used for storage areas such as rare book collections or government records and documents. If the collection is closed access, the items can be shelved in a fixed location. Advantages and disadvantages of this arrangement include:

Advantages	Disadvantages
Items are shelved in a prescribed place, and new items are added at the end of the sequence. For identification, items are given a running number or accession number (e.g., 7834, 7835, and so on). This way an item can stay in one spot in relation to other items.	Browsing is impossible because there is no subject order. Access to specific resources is gained through a catalog or finding aid.
The collection does not need to be rearranged as frequently.	Collections are not used as much as they might be as patrons may not be aware of what is held.
Space is used more economically.	
There is less wear and tear on items.	

Relative Location

Most libraries shelve their materials in a relative location, thus allowing users to browse items on the shelves. Items are generally arranged using the Dewey Decimal Classification (DDC) or Library of Congress Classification (LCC) schemes that group materials by subject. Advantages and disadvantages of this arrangement include:

Advantages	Disadvantages
New items are interfiled with old ones. As the collection expands, an item may be moved along the shelves, but it remains in the same position relative to other items.	An expanding collection can be difficult to manage because new material must be intershelved. This leads to constant shifting and the resulting costs.

Integration

In addition to decisions about the kinds of access and location, library staff also need to decide whether to integrate or segregate sections of the collection.

Total Integration (or Intershelving)

All physical library materials, regardless of their format, are shelved in one sequence. This is the ideal arrangement for a browsing collection.

Non-Integrated Shelving

All formats of resources are stored separately according to their space and equipment requirements. This is not as suitable for a browsing collection as is intershelving, but it is a practical use of space and keeps each format together to enable easy maintenance, especially for formats requiring equipment to view or use.

Partial Integration

Some materials are shelved together, especially if they have a similar format, while others are shelved separately. This is the most common option used in libraries and does allow browsing, but users need to be aware that there are other sequences they should check in order to see the library's full collection on the relevant subject.

Possible Arrangements

Parts of the collection may be arranged:

- by format (e.g., all DVDs shelved together in one sequence, oversized books on any subject all shelved together)
- in alphabetical order (e.g., fiction books arranged alphabetically by author, serials alphabetically by title)
- in numerical order (e.g., volumes within sets, a numbered series)
- in classification number order (e.g., DDC, LCC)
- by audience (e.g., young adults, graduate students)
- by lending conditions (e.g., regular circulation, reserve, noncirculating)
- by type of print (e.g., large print, braille).

EXERCISE 9.1

Arrange the following fiction books in alphabetical order by author (and title if more than one book by an author). Write the call numbers in the spaces below.

F/TRO   Trollope, Joanna. *The men and the boys.*

F/ARC   Archer, Jeffrey. *Honour among thieves.*

F/MCC   McCullough, Colleen. *The grass crown.*

F/RUS   Rushdie, Salman. *The Moor's last sigh.*

F/THE   Theroux, Paul. *My other life.*

F/TRO   Trollope, Joanna. *Next of kin.*

F/KOC   Koch, Christopher. *Highways to a war.*

F/GRI   Grisham John. *The client.*

F/KOC   Koch, Christopher. *The year of living dangerously.*

F/THE   Theroux, Paul. *The happy isles of Oceania.*

1. F/ARC	2. F/GRI	3. F/KOC Highways to a war	4. F/KOC the year of living dangerously	5. F/MCC
6. F/RUS	7. F/THE my other life	8. F/THE the happy isles of Oceania	9. F/TRO next of kin	10. F/TRO the men + the boys

Classification Schemes
Classification

In addition to arranging some of the collection by use or format, most libraries use a classification system based on subject for all or most nonfiction material. Each resource is given a call number that consists of a classification number, a book number and often a location symbol. Using the call number, clients are able to find all items on one subject together, or to locate a particular item.

Dewey Decimal Classification and Library of Congress Classification are the best known and most widely used classification schemes. Sometimes special libraries use other schemes that are more suited to arranging information for their specific client needs (e.g., Moys Classification for legal material; Pettee Classification for theological material).

Dewey Decimal Classification (DDC)

The Dewey Decimal Classification system (DDC) was created by Melvil Dewey in 1876 to 'organize all knowledge'. DDC divides all human knowledge into ten main classes, using a minimum of three digits followed by a decimal point and further digits if necessary.

The main classes are

000	Computer science, information & general works
100	Philosophy & psychology
200	Religion
300	Social sciences
400	Language
500	Science
600	Technology
700	Arts & recreation
800	Literature
900	History & geography

This is the most widely used scheme around the world, particularly in public and school libraries. Many libraries use DDC because:
- the decimal notation is simple to assign, shelve, remember and find
- the scheme is revised periodically to accommodate new topics
- widespread use of DDC and computer technology make it possible for libraries to share the work of classifying.

The DDC number represents the subject. DDC numbers are placed on the shelves in numerical order, grouping similar topics together. The digits following the decimal point are treated as decimal fractions, and would be filed on the shelf in the following order:

629
629.1
629.12
629.13
629.13092
629.132
629.1323
629.132322
629.133
629.19
629.2
629.204
629.895
630

DDC Call Numbers

Call numbers are a combination of a DDC number plus a book number or Cutter number (that represents the author's surname or the title and, sometimes, the geographic area).

Call numbers based on DDC are usually a combination of numbers and alphabetic symbols. Frequently, libraries add the first three letters of an author's name to a DDC number to create the call number:

629.13 HAN   (Author John Hanson)
629.133 THO   (Author Fay Thompson)
657.04 KEN   (Author Brian Kennedy)
658.403 BRO   (Author Amy Brown)

Optionally, libraries can use the Cutter-Sanborn tables to create a unique call number for each item, and to simplify alphabetic arrangement. Cutter-Sanborn numbers consist of the first letter of the author's name followed by numbers taken from the tables to indicate that name. Detailed instructions on how to create these numbers are included in the front of the Cutter-Sanborn tables. Using the examples above, if a library used the Cutter-Sanborn tables, the call numbers would be:

629.13 H251
629.133 T471
657.04 K35
658.403 B877

Call numbers can also indicate the location if needed (e.g., a branch of the library), a special collection to which an item belongs (e.g., reference, audiovisual) and a copy number if there is more than one copy. For example:

CITY 629.133 THO
REF 629.13 HAN
629.133 T471 Copy 3

EXERCISE 9.2

Arrange the Dewey Decimal Classification call numbers given below in numerical order. Write the numbers in the boxes.

1.

428 FRO	944 LAN	808.02 ESS	822.3 CRE
025.1 ORG	331.12 LIF	940.28 IND	302.2 COM
796.46 ATL	882.01 ANT	959.86 DON	004.1 COM
158.2 BOD	380.1 MAR	914 GRE	551.6 HOL
617.8 UND	495.6 MEE	640.42 YOU	519.5 AGA

1. 004.1 COM	2. 025.1 ORG	3. 158.2 BOD	4. 302.2 COM	5. 331.12 LIF
6. 380.1 MAR	7. 428 FRO	8. 495.6 MEE	9. 519.5 AGA	10. 551.6 HOL
11. 617.8 UND	12. 640.42 YOU	13. 796.46 ATL	14. 808.02 ESS	15. 822.3 CRE
16. 882.01 ANT	17. 914 GRE	18. 940.28 IND	19. 944 LAN	20. 959.86 DON

2.

| 027.6305 | 338.479105 | 363.960994 | 306.360941 |
| MUL | INT | SIE | HAN |

| 305.235 | 338.064 | 363.7384 | 333.33068 |
| ROS | FED | WAL | REA |

| 306.30994 | 333.333 | 027.625 | 338.476292 |
| BRE | MAL | BRO | JUR |

| 027.80994 | 338.47910904 | 363.19260973 | 305.2350994 |
| SCH | BUR | OKU | WHI |

| 333.33068 | 306.76620994 | 305.230942 | 306.380941 |
| CYR | MOD | DES | KIR |

1.	2.	3.	4.	5.
6.	7.	8.	9.	10.
11.	12.	13.	14.	15.
16.	17.	18.	19.	20.

EXERCISE 9.3

Arrange the Dewey Decimal Classification call numbers given below in numerical order for a library collection that is totally integrated (i.e., all formats intershelved).

VIDEO 332.6324 AUS	001.64404 CHO	020.6224205 LIB	158.05 JOU
052.94 AUS	SERIAL 994.020924 WAR	333.330688 CAN	614.0994 AUS
REF 614.59623 KIL	020.941 LIB	VIDEO 641.5676 LON	333.3387 SUC
005.26 BAS	SERIAL 346.9407 BUS	001.64 STA	REF 994.03 CLU
005.262 TUR	001.6404 OGD	REF 949.5074 GAG	949.5 MEN

1.	2.	3.	4.	5.
6.	7.	8.	9.	10.
11.	12.	13.	14.	15.
16.	17.	18.	19.	20.

EXERCISE 9.4

Arrange the Dewey Decimal Classification call numbers given below in numerical order, taking note of the location symbols (e.g., DVD). Arrange the numbers for a collection which has the reference materials shelved at the beginning, serials integrated with the main collection, and the DVDs shelved at the end (i.e., a segregated collection).

DVD 509.22 DON	328.73 CON	011.38 HOP	378.33 GRA
016.35471 IND	SERIAL 590.744 INT	705.8 AME	016.31 STA
REF 791.45 CON	011.6403 NEV	DVD 314.2 WHI	520.321 ENG
378.43 BAR	SERIAL 021.0025 INT	021.002541 BRI	REF 001.640321 ABR
341.2 TRI	016.35494093 GAR	DVD 020.321 HIL	REF 328.73 AUS

1.	2.	3.	4.	5.
6.	7.	8.	9.	10.
11.	12.	13.	14.	15.
16.	17.	18.	19.	20.

EXERCISE 9.5

Arrange the Dewey Decimal Classification call numbers which include Cutter-Sanborn numbers in numerical order. Write the numbers in the boxes.

364.0994 C929	364.994021 W181	364.994021 M953	364.49 C929
363.25 L131	364 H229	346.991 W587	364.994 C297
364.099 A477	364.994 A198	364.021 D562	364.99402 C444
364 B112	364.49 M476	363.25 G255	364.49 C928
364.994021 W182	363.25 M475	360 Y92	363.25 G256

1.	2.	3.	4.	5.
6.	7.	8.	9.	10.
11.	12.	13.	14.	15.
16.	17.	18.	19.	20.

Library of Congress Classification (LCC)

The Library of Congress classification system was developed by the Library of Congress to organize its own collection. Many libraries throughout the world, particularly large academic and special libraries, have adopted this classification scheme. LCC divides all human knowledge into twenty-one main classes, each identified by a single letter of the alphabet. Each main class is then further divided into subclasses by using additional letters; and numbers are used for divisions.

Subject specialists devised and continue to update the system to add new subjects. There are over 40 printed volumes in the series (which are referred to as schedules) each with its own index. The main classes are:

A	General Works
B	Philosophy. Psychology. Religion
C	Auxiliary Sciences of History
D	World History and History of Europe, Asia, Africa, Australia, New Zealand etc.
E-F	History of the Americas
G	Geography. Anthropology. Recreation
H	Social Sciences
J	Political Science
K	Law
L	Education
M	Music and Books on Music
N	Fine Arts
P	Language and Literature
Q	Science
R	Medicine
S	Agriculture
T	Technology
U	Military Science
V	Naval Science
Z	Bibliography. Library Science. Information Resources (General)

LC Call Numbers

Call numbers are a combination of the LC classification number plus the book number (or Cutter) plus the date. The Cutter represents the author's surname or the title and, sometimes, the geographic area. Call numbers usually include the date of publication. For example, two editions of Jenkinson's book on the chemistry of metals have the numbers:

QD	QD
171	171
.J47	.J47
1984	1987

Procedures for Shelving a Book by its Library of Congress Call Numbers

1. Begin with the first letter(s).

    eg   A   AC   AG   AP   B

2. After finding the proper alphabetical section, read the numbers that follow the letters in numerical order.

    eg   AP1   AP2   AP5   AP10   AP50

3. If there is a decimal point in the first row, a number to the right of the decimal point is treated as a decimal number.

    eg   DS668.29   *comes before*   DS668.3

4. Books on a similar subject have call numbers that begin with the same set of letters and numbers. Each book is then identified by the remaining letter/number set in the call number. Read the letter that begins the next line of the call number in alphabetical order.

    eg   AP2   AP2   AP2   AP2   AP2
            .A   .B   .D   .G   .S

5. Now read the final number group in the call number as a decimal number.

    eg   AP2   AP2   AP2   AP2   AP2
            .N2   .N31   .N3545   .N4   .N489

6. When a date appears as the last line of the call number, the call numbers with the additional line follow those without the date.

    eg   DS668   *comes before*   DS668
            .B39   .B39
                                       1954

7. Dates are shelved in chronological order.

    eg   JV9185.I8   *comes before*   JV9185.I8
            .C72   .C72
            1990   1996

eg **Example of Sequence**

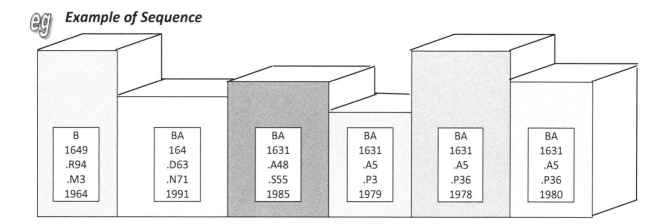

B	BA	BA	BA	BA	BA
1649	164	1631	1631	1631	1631
.R94	.D63	.A48	.A5	.A5	.A5
.M3	.N71	.S55	.P3	.P36	.P36
1964	1991	1985	1979	1978	1980

EXERCISE 9.6

Check the order of these Library of Congress Classification call numbers and list them in order.

1.

GN	GN	GN	GN	GN
325	325	324	326	326
.F47	.F7	.F531	.F5	.F5
	1979	1986	1991	1989

1.	2.	3.	4.	5.
GN 325. F47	GN 324. F531 1986	GN 325. F7 1979	GN 326.F5 1989	GN 326.F5 1991

2.

Z699.5	Z699.5	Z699.5	Z699	Z699.5
.B53	.B53	.B5	.B53	.B53
.D37	.D3	.D37	.D3	.D37
1983	1984	1985	1986	1987

1.	2.	3.	4.	5.
Z699.5 .B5.D37 1985	Z699.5 .B53.D3 1984	Z699.5 .B53.D3 1986	Z699.5 .B53.D37 1983	Z699.5 .B53.D37 1987

3.

PL2892	PL282	PL2842	PL8224	PL42
.A52	.A5	.A2	.A502	.A552
.M6	.M7	.M61	.M76	.M606
1987	1942		1990	1993

1.	2.	3.	4.	5.
PL2842 .A2. M61	PL282 .A5. M7 1942	PL2892 .A52. M6 1987	PL8224 .A502. M76 1990	PL42 .A552. M606 1993

4.

Q1
.S34

JQ4011
.E49

BF575
.S75K44

QB1
.R47

HJ2193
.S97

TX724
.5
.B47

QB86
.S35

HJ2193
.F56

BF575
.9
.A86

QL737
.C23T475

HN850
.V5A97

QB51
.A77

HJ9931
.A44

TX717
.P43

HN850
.Z9V58

JA26
.A86

HV1
.C74

GT4985
.N38

QB1
.A89441

QB1
.5
.M67

1.	2.	3.	4.	5.
6.	7.	8.	9.	10.
11.	12.	13.	14.	15.
16.	17.	18.	19.	20.

5.

QH540 .B75	Q1 .R553	DG5 .I61	HM1 .A87
HV1 .C74	T1 .226 .U54	HM1 .A5	HN850 .Z9V53
DU967 .6 .K29	Q1 .R56	HN850 .V5A97	QH540 .C38
JA26 .A86	HQ1101 .W74	QH540 .C4	QB1 .5 .M67
QH540 .C3	HN850 .Z9V58	SD1 .7 .W4	HM1 .5 .C72

1.	2.	3.	4.	5.
6.	7.	8.	9.	10.
11.	12.	13.	14.	15.
16.	17.	18.	19.	20.

6.

HT609 .S33	QP33 .5 .C3	QH511 .H35	RC632 .P56 .I57
QP34 .L348	HD5345 .A6 .C74	QH508 .G7	QP171 .S58
QA276 .8 .H34	QH508 .B3	DS611 .I44	NC1115 .B7
HT609 .R43	HV9069 .C53	PA2117 .A5	HA31 .2 .M66
HT609 .R5	JV9185 .I8 .C72	S494 .5 .W3	R127 .2 .V58

1.	2.	3.	4.	5.
6.	7.	8.	9.	10.
11.	12.	13.	14.	15.
16.	17.	18.	19.	20.

Correct Shelving Practice

To ensure users can find the library materials they need, shelvers must understand how to read the classification scheme and how to file items in the correct location. Shelving is an important process in all libraries since mis-shelved items are lost to those who are looking for them by call number.

The materials which need to be shelved include those items that have been returned from loan through the circulation desk. Other materials for shelving include:

- items that have been used in the library
- new items being added to the collection
- items returned from binding and repair
- items being transferred from one part of the collection to another.

Returning materials to their correct location as quickly as possible is a priority. Efficient reshelving of materials prevents users and staff from wasting time looking for materials not on the shelf, or from speculating whether something is missing.

Busy periods often result in shelving bottlenecks and backlogs. Designated sorting areas for materials awaiting reshelving, numbered and/or dated book trucks, or special sorting shelves on different floors can assist in keeping the shelving work flow running smoothly.

Shelving Procedure

The shelving process can be divided into several steps:

1. Sort the material by format if the library does not have a fully integrated shelving system. Categories may include:
    - reference books
    - fiction monographs
    - junior monographs
    - large print monographs
    - nonfiction monographs
    - DVDs
    - CDs
    - current periodicals
    - bound periodicals
    - microforms.

2. Sort within each format according to a broad unit - usually a range of the classification scheme. For example, sort DDC numbers by 100s, 200s, and so forth, and LCC numbers by QAs, QDs and so on.

3. Place the items on book trucks for reshelving. Arrange the items in call number order to avoid backtracking along the shelves.

4. Shelve the items.

5. Record statistics on the number of items shelved each day.

Shelving Technique

Part of the task of shelving is to ensure that the items already on the shelves are in order and in good condition. While shelving, library staff should look out for mis-shelved materials and either send them for sorting or reshelve them correctly. Materials requiring repairs and rebinding should be routed to the appropriate unit.

Shelves should be tidied constantly by:
- shifting all volumes to the left side of the shelf with a book support on the right to prevent leaning
- aligning volumes with spines to the front edge of the shelf
- relieving the pressure of items being packed too tightly by shifting one or two items to the shelf above or below.

To avoid damaging resources during shelving, try the following:
- make a space first with one hand rather than jamming resources in
- use both hands to straighten resources so that they stand upright to the left of the shelf
- carefully insert book supports to prevent damage to the base of resources.

Occupational Health and Safety (OH&S)
- Use a kick stool to work above shoulder level rather than stretching for a shelf you can barely reach.
- Sit on a kick stool when working below waist level rather than crouching or bending over.
- Pick up books with both hands rather than using one hand.
- Turn around using your feet rather than twisting your body.
- Shelve for not more than 3 hours a day.
- Try to vary tasks while shelving.
- Vary your movements while shelving and pay attention to your body as you move.
- Ensure that book trucks are evenly and not too heavily loaded because they can topple easily.

ACTIVITY 9.7

Sort a selection of library items correctly onto a trolley with spines uppermost, taking care not to jam items in. Stack the trolley observing the OH&S considerations above. Ask someone else to check your sorting before the items are shelved.

EXERCISE 9.8

Some materials require different handling because of their format. Shelve examples of each of the following formats, and comment on whether they were easier or harder to handle than books.

Material	Comparison with Shelving Books
Pamphlets	
Unbound serials	
Bound serials	
Microfiche	
Kits	
DVDs	
Maps, charts	
Newspapers	

REVISION QUIZ 9.9

Use the following questions to revise your understanding of shelving. You do not need to write down the answers.

1. What is a closed access library?

2. Why do some libraries choose to shelve their materials in a fixed location?

3. Why do libraries use a classification scheme to organize the materials on their shelves?

4. Why is it important to reshelve items promptly?

5. Give three OH&S rules you should follow when shelving.

CHAPTER TEN
Filing

Introduction

Since most library catalogs are available online, the filing of bibliographic data is done automatically. The catalog's software can generate its own lists so the need to manually file bibliographic records has been greatly reduced.

However, it is still important that we understand the principles of filing, in order to find items in lists (e.g. a bibliography), or resources shelved in alphabetical order (e.g., fiction arranged by author's surname, or serials arranged by title). Because information is organized according to a particular set of filing rules, familiarity with the rules is the most effective approach to locating information in these listings.

Library filing rules have evolved with developments in integrated library systems. When catalog cards were filed manually, the rules allowed for interpretations of the headings to be made. For example, distinctions were made between names and subjects because they were filed in separate sequences: 'St.' could be filed as if it were spelled 'Saint'. Now that most filing is done electronically, the rules need to accommodate this much more mechanical approach.

Principles of Filing

There are two basic methods for filing entries in a single sequence:
- word by word
- letter by letter.

Using one or other of these methods results in a quite different arrangement. Therefore, you must be able to recognize the basic filing arrangement in order to find a particular entry in a catalog, bibliography or listing.

Word by Word

Most library materials are filed word by word. That is, each word is filed alphabetically, but the space at the end of a word is filed before any letter. This is often referred to as the principle of 'Nothing files before something'.

 New Australians
New England cookbook
New Zealand in colour
Newbery Medal winners
Newton and gravity

Letter by Letter

Some resources are filed letter by letter (or character by character). This means that spaces between words are ignored, and each letter in each word is filed alphabetically.

 New Australians
Newbery Medal winners
New England cookbook
Newton and gravity
New Zealand in colour

ALA Filing Rules (1980)

The filing rules that libraries use were developed by the American Library Association—*ALA filing rules*, Chicago, American Library Association, 1980.

The rules are intended to apply to the arrangement of bibliographic records regardless of the cataloging rules by which the records have been created.

The main rules are summarized below. For any filing situations not covered here, consult the full text of the 1980 *ALA filing rules*.

The basic filing order is word by word.

 New Zealand in colour
Newbery Medal winners

The rules use the 'file-as-is' principle. File an entry as it looks rather than as it sounds.

 Miss Read
Misunderstood in Miami
Mr. Chips

No distinction is made between different types of headings. Therefore, personal names, corporate names, titles and subject headings are all interfiled in the same sequence.

 Archer, Jeffrey
Architects Anonymous
ARCHITECTURE
Architecture and design in Australia

The principle of 'nothing before something' applies, so a space (or equivalent) is regarded as nothing.

 S E C
Sally Kelly

Dashes, hyphens, diagonal slashes, and periods are all regarded as equivalent to a space or 'nothing'. However if any of the above precede the first character in an element they are ignored.

   AAP Reuters
- angry young men
Apres vous

O, Chae-ho
O.E.C.D.
OAU/STRC
OAU today

Upper and lower case letters are equivalent.

   ARCHITECTURE
Architecture and design
ARCHITECTURE--FRANCE

All entries beginning with numbers are arranged before entries beginning with letters. Numbers are filed in numerical order.

   16 : Heaven or Hell?
44 short poems
101 ways to get a job
AAP Reuters

Numbers that are spelled out interfile with other entries in alphabetical order.

   Ferguson, John
Fifty-five days in Peking
Forty-four nursery rhymes
FRANCE

Punctuation used to increase readability in numbers (e.g., 2,730) is ignored.
Other punctuation (e.g., 1948/49) is treated as a space.

   10/3 a date to remember
101 uses for a dead cat
1,001 years in space

Initial articles that are an integral part of personal or place names (e.g., El Greco, Las Vegas) are included in filing.

   Long Island
Los Angeles
Louisiana

Initial articles at the **beginning** of title, series and subject entries (e.g., a, an, the, and their equivalents in other languages) are ignored.

    West, John
The West Sports Association
The western adventure
A western film

Articles in the middle of a heading are filed in the same way as any other word.

    West is best
West is better than North
West is the best

Initials, initialisms and acronyms are filed as they appear in the entry. If they are written with spaces, dashes, hyphens, diagonal slashes or periods between letters (e.g., L.A.A., S E C) file each letter as a separate word. If they appear as a word (e.g., JPEG) or have letters separated by symbols other than those mentioned above (e.g., P*E*R*T*), they are filed as words.

    F.F.B.
Father Time

Hum and be happy
H*Y*M*A*N K*A*P*L*A*N
Hymns of praise

U.N. or World War III?
Uncontrolled joy
UNESCO
Unicef
United Arab Republic

A prefix that is written as a separate word at the beginning of a personal or place name (e.g., De Alberti) is treated as a separate word.

    Da Ponti
Dante
De Alberti
De La Fontaine
Dean
Debrett

A prefix that is joined to the rest of the name directly or by an apostrophe without a space (e.g., D'Arcy, Maclaren) is filed as part of the name.

    Da Trevi
Daniel
D'Arcy
Dastardly deeds in Dundee

With the exception for dashes, hyphens, diagonal slashes and periods, and the special rules for numbers, all punctuation and nonalphabetic symbols are ignored in filing.

 $$$ and sense
Andrew ***, Baron of Styx
Andrew/Sarah/Eugenie/Beatrice
Andrew Windsor, the last monarch?
Andr*w, son of Elizabeth

Common abbreviations, signs and symbols are arranged as if they were spelled out in full. (However, the way that Mrs. is filed is an exception to this rule.)

 Doctor at sea
Dr. Christian's office
Doctor come quickly
Doktor Brents Wandlung

Names that begin with Mc, M' and Mac are arranged as if they were written as Mac.

 Mach
McHenry
Machinery
MacHugh
Machuron
Maclaren, Ian
M'Laren, J. Wilson
McLaren, Jack
MacLaren, James

 How to File: a Summary

Whether we are filing an alphabetical list or shelving resources alphabetically, the conventions that we use follow the *ALA Filing Rules*. The key points for filing are:

1. Arrangement is word by word, alphabetizing letter by letter to the end of each word.
2. Numbers are filed in numerical order. Spelled out numbers are interfiled in alphabetical order.
3. Punctuation is treated as a space.
4. When the first word of a title is an article (a, an, or the), it is disregarded in the filing. This is also true of articles in foreign languages.
5. When an article is within a title, it is observed in the filing.
6. Initials are arranged before a word beginning with the same letter.
7. Names with prefixes. (De, De la, La, Las, O', Van, Von, etc.) Personal and place names compounded with prefixes are treated as one word.
8. Names beginning with M' and Mc are filed as though they were spelled Mac.
9. Common abbreviations are arranged as though they were spelled out (except for Mrs).
10. Hyphenated words are filed as two words.

ACTIVITY 10.1
Examine the list below, and be sure that you understand the filing position of each entry. Refer again to the above rules for any arrangement you are not sure of.

7 little Australians	MACALISTER RIVER
10/3 a date to remember	MacAlister, Stephen
16 : Heaven or Hell?	Macdonald
44 short poems	McDonald, Peter
101 uses for a dead cat	Machinery
1,001 years in space	Mack the knife
AAP Reuters	Miss Read
$$$ and sense	Misunderstood in Miami
Andrew ***, Baron of Styx	Mr. Chips
Andrew/Sarah/Eugenie/Beatrice	New England cookbook
Andrew Windsor, the last monarch?	Newbery Medal winners
Andr*w, son of Elizabeth	O, Chae-ho
- angry young men	O.E.C.D.
Apres vous	OAU/STRC
Architects Anonymous	OAU today
Architecture and design in Australia	S E C
ARCHITECTURE--FRANCE	S.P.C.A.
Da Ponti	Sally Kelly
Dante	Senatorship
D'Arcy	SINGAPORE
Dastardly deeds in Dundee	* The Society to Outlaw Pornography
De Alberti	Spencer, Andrew
De La Fontaine	SPUD : let's prevent unwholesome diets
Dean	U.N. or World War III?
F.F.B.	Uncontrolled joy
Ferguson, John	UNESCO
Fifty-five days in Peking	Unicef
Forty-four nursery rhymes	United Arab Republic
FRANCE	UNITED NATIONS – BIBLIOGRAPHY
Hum and be happy	The United Nations in the 20th century
H*Y*M*A*N K*A*P*L*A*N	UNITED STATES -- THE WEST
Hymns of praise	The United States under Reagan
Long Island	THE WEST
Los Angeles	West, John
Louisiana	The West Sports Association
Mac Donald, John	A western adventure

EXERCISE 10.2

File the following sets of entries word by word, using the 1980 ALA filing rules. (Hint: If you have difficulty filing, write each word of the exercise on a separate card. Practice filing the cards until you are confident, then complete the exercises in the book.)

1.

Air conditioning

Air cushion vehicles

Airports

Air transport

Air and space resources

Aircraft

Air pollution

Air Force

Airfields

Air, Lesley

2.

Gone is gone

Go tell it on the mountain

Gold fever

Gondolas of Venose

Golden girls

Good housekeeping

Goody Townhouse

Good wives

Go down Moses

Goannas

Gold and silver

Golf for amateurs

Goodness gracious me

Goodbye cruel world

Gold mining

3.

English men of literature

England and the near east

Englische dogges

English historical documents

Engines and trains

Englishmen

Engineers unlimited

English literature

The enigma of drug addiction

Englisch Sprechen!

4.

Approach to housing

A is for alphabet

Danger on the ski trails

That's the way

The language laboratory

The laundry basket

Label manufacturing

An April After

Archaeology and Old Testament

A Lexicon of the German language

Lexicon of jargon

That was summer

The labour gang

The labrador puppies

Ladders and snakes

An Approach to Hamlet

That's me

The Acts

The Danger of Equality

The Archaeology of Carajou

5.

Twenty poems

Twenty and two

$12 to May

20% profit

Twelve angry jelly beans

Twenty soldiers

12 x 8 : Paper read to the Crown Club

Twelve drunk teddy bears

20 + 20 = 40

20/- change

 EXERCISE 10.3

Here are some of the exercises you have just filed word by word. Now file each set letter by letter.

1.

Air conditioning

Air cushion vehicles

Airports

Air transport

Air and space resources

Aircraft

Air pollution

Air Force

Airfields

Air, Lesley

2.

English men of literature

England and the near east

Englische dogges

English historical documents

Engines and trains

Englishmen

Engineers unlimited

English literature

Enigma of drug addiction

Englisch Sprechen!

3.

Gone is gone

Go tell it on the mountain

Gold fever

Gondolas of Venose

Golden girls

Good housekeeping

Goody Townhouse

Good wives

Go down Moses

Goannas

Gold and silver

Golf for amateurs

Goodness gracious me

Goodbye cruel world

Gold mining

EXERCISE 10.4

The following lists are in correct alphabetical order. For each list, decide whether the order is word by word, or letter by letter. State briefly how you recognised the order.

1.
Cape Cod Bay
Cape Dyer
Cape Jervis
Capel
Capela de Campo
Capel Curig
Capella, Mt.
Cape Preston
Capetown
Cape Virtue

The order is_____

I recognised the order by _____

_____

_____

2.
File extensions
File menu
File - print command
File - save as command
Files – assembling
Files – MIDI
Find program
Find tab (Help program)
Finding - Hidden windows
Floppy discs

The order is_____

I recognised the order by _____

_____

_____

3.
C:\> prompt. *See* Dos prompt
CD player
CD-ROM drives
CD-ROM viewing
CD-ROMs. *See* Compact Discs
Control panel
Controls
Ctrl key
Free form select tool
FreeCell

The order is_____

I recognised the order by _____

_____

_____

4.
Hawker, R.
Hawker Roofing
Hawker's Barry Butchery
Hawker Self Serve
Hawker Tennis Centre
Hawkes, Adrian J.
Hawkesbury Constructions
Hawkes Butchery
Hawkins, Jimmy
Hawkinson Self Serve

The order is_____

I recognised the order by _____

_____

_____

EXERCISE 10.5
Use the ALA filing rules to arrange each of these bibliographies in correct word by word order. Take care to transcribe each citation accurately.

1.

Plasketes, George. *B-Sides, Undercurrents and overtones : peripheries to popular in music, 1960 to the present,* Burlington, Ashgate, 2009.

Hitchins, Ray, *Vibe merchants : the sound creators of Jamaican popular music,* Burlington, VT Ashgate, 2014.

Rechniewski, Peter, 'The permanent underground: Australian contemporary jazz in the new millennium', *Platform Papers*, No. 16, 2008, pages 1-59.

Zak, Albin J. III, *I don't sound like nobody: remaking music in 1950s*, Ann Arbor, University of Michigan Press, 2010.

Baker, Sarah Louise, Bennett, Andy and Taylor, Jodie Louise, *Redefining mainstream popular music*, http//www.routledge.com/books/details/9780415807821/, 2013-06-21.

Spicer, Mark and John Covach, *Sounding out pop : analytical essays in popular music,* Ann Arbor, University of Michigan Press, 2010.

Cardany, Audrey Berger, 'Music activities for 'Lemonade in Winter'', *General Music Today*, vol. 27, no. 2, January 2014, page 36.

Garofalo, Reebee, *Rockin' out : Popular music in the U.S.A.*, Upper Saddle River, Pearson, 2014.

Toft, Robert, *Hits and misses : crafting top 40 singles, 1963-1971*, New York, Continuum, 2010.

Everett, Walter, *Expression in pop-rock music*, 2nd ed. New York, Routledge, 2008.

2.

IEEE transactions on information technology, New York, Institute of Engineers, 1955.

I.T.: journal of information technology, Sydney, Macquarie University, 1995-

Access: the supplementary index to Internet serials, Washington, DC, Gaylord, 1975-

IEEE transactions on computers, New York, Institute of Electrical and Electronics Engineers, 1959-

IEEE/ACM transactions on networking, New York, Institute of Electrical and Electronics Engineers and the Association for Computing Machinery, 22:3, June 2014.

IEEE transactions on communications, New York, Institute of Electrical and Electronics Engineers, 62:4, April 2014.

IEEE annals of the history of computing, Los Alamitos, Calif., IEEE Computer Society, 1979-

IEEE and The Open Group. 'Standard for Information Technology—Portable Operating System Interface (POSIX®)', *Base Specifications,* Issue 7, *2013.* Digital file.

I.B.M. journal of research and development, New York, International Business Machines Corporation, 54: 2, 2010.

Information sources in information technology, editor, David Haynes, London, de Gruyter Saur, 2013. Digital file.

EXERCISE 10.6
The following list of serials is in correct ALA filing rules order.

24 hours: ABC FM program
Abridged reader's guide to periodical literature
Booklist
Bulletin of the Centre for Children's Books
CSIRO papers
Defense abstracts
Four to fourteen
The horn book magazine
A journal of documentation
Mt Isa Mines ecological quarterly
Queensland. Department of Education. Annual report
Sociofile

Interfile the following into the list above.

The bulletin
Mount Morgan mining review
Social science abstracts
Book review digest
4 weekly poets
Defence index
3rd world report
The journal of early childhood behaviour
C.S.R. quarterly report
Queensland agricultural review

EXERCISE 10.8 (OPTIONAL)

These entries are in order. Examine them, and decide the filing principles used. (This exercise is challenging. If you have difficulty, check the answers in the back of the book, or consult a teacher or supervisor.)

150 masterpieces of drawing
114 ways to be your own boss
112 2nd form students
One hundred and two H bombs
One single minute
1050 jewellery designs
'39 to '94: the years of change
3000 elephants in a Mini?
3111 buttons
3001: the year of the future
20th century Britain
Twentieth century drama

The filing principles are _____

_____

Now interfile the following items.

1001 fishing trips
100 ideas for the pianist
Twelve lesson course
12 noon
The Twentieth century
One two buckle my shoe
One Australia
106 funny things
One thousand and one nights
150,000 years
160 feet down
3010 pieces of paper
3101 feet of rope
113 teams of netball players
30 bald heads
100,000 jelly beans in a bag
3001 days to blast off

CHAPTER ELEVEN
Damage and Repairs

Introduction
A prime task for library staff is to prevent damage to the materials stored by the library. The damage may be caused by:
- incorrect handling by library users or staff
- environmental factors
- the composition of the materials.

Causes of Damage
Manual Handling
People are often described as the worst enemies of library materials, because they cause so much damage intentionally and unintentionally.
- **Library users** often overuse or abuse materials, especially books: by using paper clips, pins or staples to mark their place; by pressing on spines when photocopying; by folding over the corners of pages; by spilling food and drinks; by making pencil marks; or simply by handling materials roughly.
- **Library staff** also cause damage by carrying too many items and dropping them; by overloading book trucks; by forcing items onto tightly-packed shelves; by using inappropriate repair techniques; and so forth.
- **Library storage can be inadequate**. Each type of material needs to be considered differently, and each must be provided with its own arrangements, support and protection.

Environment
- **Light:** Sunlight bleaches covers of books, fades colors in maps and prints, harms paper, and fades microform. Artificial light, particularly fluorescent lighting, is damaging to many library materials. On the other hand, dark surroundings encourage infestations of insects, rodents and fungi.
- **Temperature:** Heat makes materials brittle. If materials have been stored in a cold area, condensation occurs when they are moved to warmer surroundings.
- **Humidity:** Mold and fungi grow if the air is too humid, but if the air is too dry some library materials dry out (e.g., paper becomes brittle).
- **Atmosphere:** Sulphur dioxide in the air forms sulphuric acid that causes brittleness in paper and decomposes leather. Hydrogen sulphide, ammonia, ozone, nitrogen oxides and aerosols may also cause damage.
- **Pests:** Insects such as silverfish and woodworms cause damage to library materials and equipment. Rats and mice eat and/or make nests in library material.

Composition of the Materials
Various components in library materials sometimes cause damage. For example, the acid in newsprint leads to the rapid deterioration of newspapers.

Preventing or Alleviating Damage
Manual Handling
- Libraries need to educate library users and their own staff in the correct handling of physical resources in order to prevent overuse and abuse of the collection. It may be necessary to restrict access to more valuable or fragile materials, and substitute originals with copies.
- Library staff should be instructed in the correct techniques for repairing and covering materials.

Environment
- The library needs to monitor lighting and ensure it is not too bright and not too dark. For example, it should control sunlight and monitor fluorescent light.
- It is important to check humidity to ensure the air is not too dry and not too damp and to make sure that air circulates throughout the collection. The ideal environment has steady relative humidity (55%) and a steady temperature (70ºF or 21ºC).
- To minimize stress from temperature changes and moisture condensation, discs should be stored at a temperature similar to that of the area where they are to be used.
- It may be necessary to fumigate the library to destroy pests. Be careful, however, that the chemicals used are not harmful to the library materials.

Composition of the Materials
- In order to prolong the life of library materials, some libraries protect them with packaging such as boxes, folders, jackets or special storage systems.
- Library staff should clean shelves and materials regularly and ensure that materials are not packed together too tightly.

Some libraries choose an alternative form of publication to preserve the intellectual content of their materials. These methods include:
- scanning or digitizing
- microfilming
- recording (e.g., talking books)
- entering information into a database.

Scanning and Digitizing
Scanning and digitizing are the preferred methods for preserving the intellectual content of resources. They have many advantages over other methods, including:
- less space is needed to store digital media, as the equivalent of volumes of monographs can be placed on one disc or file
- resources can be distributed more easily once they are in electronic form
- finding a specific portion within a resource is quicker, as you can jump to different sections more easily.

This has led to a significant increase in the number of existing resources being converted into digital formats. CDs and DVDs are the most popular choices for recording and storing all types of digital content.

Archiving resources in this way also ensures the resource will be available into the future, as it helps prevent intellectual content being lost through disaster, theft or mishandling.

ACTIVITY 11.1
Visit a library and look closely at any group of 10 monographs on any shelf. Fill in the number of monographs fitting each category.

Damage to monographs	Yes	No
Are the covers in good condition?		
Are the spines damaged?		
Is the damage at the top or base of the spines?		
Are the spines loose?		
Are there any loose pages?		
Are the corners of pages folded over?		
Are there pen or pencil marks on the pages?		
Is the text underlined or highlighted?		
Are there any torn pages?		
Is there any evidence of repair (e.g., taped spines , sticky tape)?		

ACTIVITY 11.2

Visit a library and make comments on the following points:

The environment	
Temperature	
Light	
Cleanliness (any dust, pests?)	
The shelving	
Is it crowded?	
Are the materials in order?	
Do library staff or the users reshelve?	
Protection of materials	
What methods are used?	
Are they effective?	
Access to digital resources	
Does the library's website have any broken links?	

Do you think the collection is well maintained based on the status of the shelves, the ambient temperature, etc.?

ACTIVITY 11.3

*Choose **two** examples of non-print materials and examine them for damage. Describe the nature of the damage, explain the factors which have caused it and suggest ways of preventing these types of damage.*
Write the details in the table below.

Damage to non-print materials	Example 1	Example 2
Item		
Nature of the damage		
What caused the damage?		
How could you prevent this damage?		

Library Rules

Libraries make their collections available for all patrons. Each library establishes rules which will allow patrons and staff to use their facilities and collections in an equitable way.

Generally, library rules will fall into the following categories, that allow staff to:

- maintain access to the library's collection and facilities
- ensure the personal safety and comfort of staff and users
- appropriately allocate staff resources.

The following rules were given to users of a research library to ensure that they handled the library materials correctly.

LIBRARY RULES

Warning

This research library aims to provide its clients with the information they require to complete their research. We try to make all materials available for your use, but this depends on how our clients handle the materials. You are asked to handle materials carefully and to take note of the following rules:

1.   Do not handle the books roughly.
2.   Do not drop the books or leave them on the floor.
3.   Do not write in the books.
4.   Do not eat or drink while in the library.
5.   Do not turn over or fold the pages in the books.
6.   Do not lean on the books when photocopying.
7.   Do not place books on top of each other.
8.   Do not use pens as bookmarks.
9.   Do not cut out or tear any of the pages.
10.   Please return books to the book truck when you have finished.

EXERCISE 11.4

Describe how you think a client might react when given these rules. Can you suggest any improvements?

ACTIVITY 11.5

Prepare a list of guidelines for a new member of the library staff on the correct handling of library materials.

Repairs

All library staff should be on the lookout for items that need repair or rebinding. Staff notice damaged items while shelving materials, when materials are returned from loan, during shelf reading and when doing an inventory (or stocktaking). Library users may also point out damage. Repairs or rebinding should be done as soon as possible to avoid further damage. The main objective of repairing materials is to keep them available for use.

If an item is damaged, there are several options:
- repairing
- rebinding
- repackaging
- discarding if badly damaged
- replacing.

Library staff complete simple repairs such as replacing spine labels, reinforcing torn or loose spines, replacing loose pages, repairing torn pages and removing paper clips or other page markers. More difficult repairs are likely to be done by specialist staff, or the items may be sent to a commercial binding firm. If the person who discovers the damage does not have the necessary skill to complete the repair, the task should be assigned to someone who can do it properly.

Simple repairs can be carried out in-house, using materials purchased from library suppliers. A wide range of tapes are available to mend torn pages, repair damaged spines and attach covers or casings. Special adhesives are available for replacing loose pages or for re-attaching covers of paperbacks and spines of hardback books.

If the library staff are too busy to repair an item immediately, they should place a slip of paper in the item with a description of the damage and set it aside. They should also enter a note in the library catalog to indicate that the item will not be found on the shelf (e.g., 'Item being repaired').

Repair, Rebind or Discard?

Library staff may need to decide whether it is worthwhile to spend the time repairing an item, to send it for rebinding, or to discard it. When making this decision, the following questions should be considered:
- Is the item needed immediately by a library user?
- Does the library hold other copies of the item?
- Is it possible to purchase a replacement?
- Can the library afford to buy a replacement?
- Is the item still in demand or only used infrequently?
- Is the information available in a different format?
- How serious is the damage?
- Does the library have the equipment and supplies needed to repair the damage?
- Is the item out of date?
- Does the item belong to a special collection?
- Is the item rare or valuable?

If the decision is made to discard the item, the library catalog must be updated to record this information.

Rebinding

Collection maintenance staff need to decide whether they are able to repair an item themselves, or whether they should send it to a bindery. In some cases, the cost of rebinding might be too high so the library staff will either discard the item or try to mend it themselves.

If you decide to rebind an item, you need to prepare detailed binding instructions. You should include information on the author, title and call number as well as details on the type of binding required, style of lettering, etc. It is important to update the catalog record to let users know the item is at the bindery and to adjust the record when the item returns to the shelves.

Binding of Serials

Even though most serial titles held by libraries are electronic, print serials (particularly older titles) are still held. Many libraries prolong the life of their print serial collections by binding several issues together. This ensures that the issues stay in logical order and are protected from damage.

When preparing serials for binding, library staff sort the issues into binding order, examine the issues for damage, locate missing issues, add indexes, title pages, and supplements if required, and complete a set of instructions for the bindery.

The library maintains a binding record that includes information describing:
- which serial titles are bound
- how often a serial is bound and how many issues are in a volume
- whether the serial has a separate index that is to be included
- the form of the title and volume numbers to be printed on the spine
- the color of the binding and type of material used
- special instructions such as whether to include the advertisements.

When the serials return from the bindery, library staff check that all of the instructions have been carried out, and amend the library records to show that the serials have been bound and are back in the library. The serials are then processed and returned to the shelves.

EXERCISE 11.6

Examine a number of damaged items in different formats (e.g., monographs, serials, DVDs etc.) and consider:

Question	Item 1	Item 2	Item 3
1. What caused the damage?			
2. Could it be fixed in a library or does it need special treatment?			
3. Is the item worth keeping?			
4. Has past mending caused further damage?			

EXERCISE 11.7

Look in a library supplier's catalog and read about the products used for repair.

1. Examine three monographs and describe what action you would take to repair each area of damage, including what material you would use. For example: 'Glue in loose pages individually using a brush and adhesive.'

Damage	Action
1.	
2.	
3.	

2. At the following link *http://www.raeco.com.au/keeping_books_alive_guide* watch the book covering and repair demonstration videos. Then complete the following repairs on materials from your library or your own collection:
    a torn page
    a loose page
    a torn cover
    a broken spine
    a damaged or tattered spine
    a spine which has separated from the book.

3. Examine three DVDs or CDs and describe what action you would take to repair each area of damage, including what material you would use. Look out for:
    damage caused by exposure to excess heat or moisture
    damage caused by light
    scratches on the laser reading side of the CD or DVD
    damage to outer case.

Damage	Action
1.	
2.	
3.	

4. Examine examples of other non-print materials, and describe the damage which is likely to occur to them. Describe how you would repair these items.

Likely Damage	Action
1.	
2.	
3.	

REVISION QUIZ 11.8

Use the following questions to revise your understanding of damage and repairs.
You do not need to write down the answers.

1. How does a library prevent damage caused by people handling the resources?

2. Describe three features of the ideal environment for preventing damage to library materials.

3. Why is it important to repair damaged materials promptly?

4. Describe four factors that library staff need to consider when deciding whether an item is worth repairing.

5. Why do many libraries bind their serials?

CHAPTER TWELVE
Inventory

Introduction
The inventory process (also known as stocktaking) enables a library to produce an accurate measure of its physical collection. When taking inventory of the material, the staff check for missing items by comparing the library's holdings with:
- the material on the shelves
- lists of the material on loan
- lists of the material at the bindery
- other information that accounts for why physical resources are not on the shelf during the inventory.

Why Libraries Do Inventory
The major reasons why a library would conduct an inventory include:
- meeting audit requirements. Libraries could be required to account for property (including equipment and supplies) and materials; and to ensure that correct financial controls apply.
- finding out how many items are missing and which areas of the collection are most affected. A library may need to improve its security arrangements if a large proportion of items are missing.
- assessing the condition of the collection and setting aside items for repair or rebinding.
- preparing for a major project such as the upgrade of the circulation system or the catalog.
- evaluating the strengths and weaknesses of the collection. Gaps or excesses in the collection can be identified by analyzing the collection in call number order.

Main Methods of Inventory
Complete
This is a major task, usually only done by small libraries (e.g., school libraries) or by larger libraries that are having serious problems caused by inaccurate records.

The process involves:
- recalling as many loans as possible. An amnesty may encourage users to return late items. Items urgently needed by users may then be released after sighting and recording.
- shelf reading to ensure the collection is in good shelf order.
- comparing items on the shelf to the shelflist, if the library maintains one, and noting any missing items.

- comparing missing items with binding files, the repair collection, and the list of materials held in storage.
- treating the remaining items as missing, and searching for them in offices, on desks, etc.
- identifying problems such as materials with no records, duplicate copies not noted, records but no materials, and then giving the details to the cataloging section so they can amend the records.
- withdrawing catalog records for missing items after an exhaustive search and adjusting other records to identify items as missing. Some libraries record the items as missing on the record and wait until the next inventory before removing the record, in case the item is found later.

Continuous
This involves doing an inventory of one section of the library at a time. Using this method, it may take many years to complete an inventory of the whole collection.

The advantages with this approach are:
- most of the library resources are available to users
- material on short loan is not recalled
- lower concentration of staff time is required
- work in other areas of the library is not disrupted
- problems arrive in the technical services section in smaller batches, causing minimal disruption to other work.

A problem with this method occurs when books are shelved incorrectly, so an efficient shelf reading program must exist if continuous inventory is to be effective.

Pilot or Sample
This involves sampling the whole collection (e.g., every 100th book). The percentage of the collection sampled depends on the accuracy of the information required—the larger the sample, the greater the accuracy.

This technique is used:
- to decide whether a full inventory is needed
- to achieve a reasonable indication of the loss rate and thereby to evaluate security or purchasing policy
- to determine which areas of the library may need a full inventory.

Scanned
The fastest way to conduct an inventory is to scan the barcodes on the items while they are on the shelves, using a portable scanner or wand. If you have to conduct a manual inventory, a great deal of time is spent taking each item off the shelf and matching it against the shelflist. With a scanned inventory the details of the item are electronically matched, and the system records the location of the item. Library staff then prepare a list of any items not out on loan and not found on the shelves. These items are recorded as lost.

Shelflist

A shelflist is the record of the resources in a library. Items in the shelflist are arranged in the same order as the resources on the shelves.

Before automation, one card from each set of catalog cards was filed in the shelflist, which was accessible only to library staff. It was used:

- to guide classifiers as to the use of a particular number
- to check the most recent allocation of book numbers if the library used unique call numbers
- to show classifiers which numbers were used previously, to maintain consistency
- as an aid to collection development, to show the strengths, weaknesses and gaps in the collection
- as an inventory record, for stocktaking
- as a historical and statistical record of the collection
- as an insurance record
- to provide subject bibliographies for reference staff.

Almost all these functions can be performed by an online catalog, and increasingly libraries do not maintain a separate shelflist:

- The need for a unique call number is reduced, since in most online systems the circulation records are controlled by a separate barcode.
- Stocktaking (where it still occurs) is done by reading the barcodes on the items with a wand, and using the online system to compare this information with its database.
- Classification numbers can be checked directly from the catalog.
- Subject bibliographies can be produced by the system.
- In an online system, each item has only one record with several access points, compared with the several cards for each item in a card catalog. Therefore the catalog is an accurate historical and statistical record and inventory, provided that it is backed up regularly and a backup copy is stored off-site.

Where libraries continue to maintain a separate shelflist, consideration must be given to its usefulness, compared with the cost of maintaining it.

Shelf Reading

Many libraries do not do inventories because of the costs involved but they may shelf read to ensure the collection is in order. The purpose of shelf reading is different, however, because it is intended merely to ensure that the items which are in the library are in the correct order on the shelf.

EXERCISE 12.1

The catalog record below is for an item which is missing from a library collection. Do you think the library staff should delete the record rather than mark the item as missing? Give reasons for your decision.

You searched for the AUTHOR: james marianne	
TITLE	Crime prevention for older Australians / Marianne Pinkerton James.
AUTHOR	James, Marianne Pinkerton.
EDITION	1st ed.
PUBLISHED	Canberra : Australian Institute of Criminology, 1993.
DESCRIPT	ix, 79 p.: ill. ; 22 cm.
SUBJECT	Crime prevention - Australia.
BIBLIOG.	Bibliography: p. 75-79.
ISBN	0642186316

LOC'N	CALL No.	STATUS
1. Central library	362.88 JAM	Missing

Weeding

Weeding (or de-selecting) is the process of discarding library materials. The decision to weed may result from an inventory or it may be a continuous process. Weeding is often a response to a special need, particularly if a section of the library has become very crowded, leaving no room for new materials. Many libraries have a weeding policy that is part of the collection development policy.

Reasons for Weeding

- information is out of date or inaccurate
- material is worn out physically
- better materials are available
- duplicate copies are found in the collection
- the item has not been used or borrowed for a long time
- community needs and/or the curriculum have changed
- institutional objectives have changed, thereby changing the library's objectives
- unwanted material has contributed to overcrowded, untidy shelves that are difficult to use.

Other ways of reducing the size of the collection include:

- using compact storage or offsite storage for little-used materials
- reformatting resources (e.g., digitizing to store information)
- limiting the subject areas of the collection or assigning some specializations to other libraries.

Deciding What to Weed

Many libraries have a written weeding policy that gives clear guidelines on what materials should be weeded. Library staff examine each item to determine whether it fits the guidelines. The final decision on whether to discard an item is usually made by the professional staff who often ask for advice from knowledgeable clients.

When material has been removed from the open shelves, it may be stored in closed stacks, in compact shelving or at a remote location; it may be disposed of in a sale or auction; or discarded. Some libraries prepare duplicates lists offering the unwanted items to other libraries. This is useful for libraries wishing to build up collections in new subject areas, or trying to obtain out-of-print materials.

For example, the Duplicate Exchange Union (DEU), operated by the American Library Association, acts as a clearinghouse that arranges for the exchange of publications deemed surplus by one library but needed by another.

The final stage of weeding involves removing all records of items that have been discarded, or recording the transfer of relocated materials. The records that must be amended include the catalog, guides to the library, financial records, and the item itself (if it is being relocated rather than discarded).

Weeding Criteria

For some libraries the weeding criteria is based on qualitative decisions. The acronym MUSTIE is a useful way to determine the qualitative weeding criteria. MUSTIE stands for:

- **M**isleading—factually inaccurate
- **U**gly—worn beyond mending
- **S**uperseded—new edition or better information available
- **T**rivial—no literary or scientific merit
- **I**rrelevant—to needs of the library
- **E**lsewhere—material easily borrowed or available from another source.

Some libraries base their weeding decisions on quantitative criteria using numerical or statistical measurements. In these instances the criteria used could include:

- date of publication
- published before a certain date
- borrowing statistics
- usage over a specified period of time
- last usage
- a combination of these.

More commonly, libraries develop a weeding policy that includes a combination of qualitative and quantitative weeding criteria.

Example of a Weeding Policy

<table>
<tr><td></td><td></td></tr>
<tr><td></td><td></td></tr>
<tr><td></td><td></td></tr>
<tr><td></td><td></td></tr>
<tr><td></td><td></td></tr>
</table>

EXERCISE 12.2

Answer the following questions relating to the Downtown College Library weeding guidelines:

1. Do you agree with weeding all books which have not been borrowed in the last three years? Can you think of any problems associated with implementing this guideline?

2. How would the library staff keep up-to-date with changes in the curriculum?

3. How would library staff decide whether a book was heavily used?

4. Why has the library decided to give preference to non-print formats of reference materials?

5. Why does the library keep only the most recent edition of reference books in the reference collection?

6. How would library staff check the physical condition of the audiovisual materials?

7. Why is the media department consulted about the cost-effectiveness of repairing audiovisual materials?

8. Why does the library check to see whether another library holds a serial before cancelling a title?

9. Why does the policy include visual observation as a measure of serial use?

REVISION QUIZ 12.3

Use the following questions to revise your understanding of inventory. You do not need to write down the answers.

1. Why do most libraries decide not to inventory the complete collection at once?

2. What is a shelflist?

3. Why is it important to shelf read the collection before doing an inventory?

4. Why do libraries weed their collections?

5. What types of materials are most likely to be weeded from a collection?

ANSWERS

EXERCISE 1.1

Indicate which library section or department (i.e. Technical Services or Public Services) would be most likely to do the tasks listed in the table below.

Library Task	Library Department
Shelving	Public Services
Promotion and Display	Public Services
Circulation	Public Services
Reader Education	Public Services
Acquisitions	Technical Services
Cataloging	Technical Services
Reference Service	Public Services
Final Processing	Technical Services
Collection Maintenance	Public Services

REVISION QUIZ 1.2

1. *What skills are needed by someone working in a library?*
   Staff working in a library need:
   - technical skills to organize and access the information
   - communication skills to help patrons use the information.

2. *What are the benefits of electronic resources?*
   For library users electronic information is beneficial because information is provided:
   - faster
   - at any time (not just when the library is open)
   - more conveniently, as access to resources may be available from home or in the library or anywhere else by means of a computer.
   Electronic resources are beneficial to libraries because the resources:
   - don't take up valuable space on shelves
   - can't be stolen or destroyed
   - allow more than one user to access information at the same time (if the license allows it).

3. *Give three examples of the following types of resources:*
   Your answers could include the following:
   a. *Audio*
      Audiocassettes, CDs, MP3 files, playaway, sound track reels, streamed audio files, recorded readings, recitations, speeches, interviews, oral histories, computer-generated speech, etc.
   b. *Electronic*
      E-book, electronic journal, MP3, online pdf, streaming video, streaming music, digital image, website
   c. *Images*
      Film cartridges, film cassettes, film reels, film rolls, filmstrips, overhead transparencies, slides, maps, remote-sensing images, satellite images, drawings, paintings, diagrams, photographic images

d. *Text*

Book, CD containing text, e-book, electronic journal, online pdf, manuscript, large print book

EXERCISE 2.1

1.

Title	The oil man and the sea: navigating the northern gateway
Author, editors, compilers, translators, illustrators, etc.	Arno Kopecky, Trena White, Ilja Herb
Place(s) of publication	Madeira Park, BC
Name of publisher(s)	Douglas & McIntyre
Copyright date	2013
Edition, if any	
Physical characteristics	264 pages, map, photographs
Series (if any)	
Notes	
Standard number(s)	ISBN 9781771001076

2.

Title	Snow falling on cedars
Author, editors, compilers, translators, illustrators, etc.	Ron Bass, Scott Hicks, Kathleen Kennedy
Place(s) of publication	New York
Name of publisher(s)	Newmarket Press
Copyright date	1999
Edition, if any	First edition
Physical characteristics	166 pages, illustrations, 24 cm
Series (if any)	Newmarket Shooting Script Series
Notes	A screenplay Based on the novel by David Guterson
Standard number(s)	ISBN 1557043728

EXERCISE 2.2

1. a. What punctuation mark separates the title from the author statement?

A diagonal slash separates the title and author statements.

b. What punctuation mark is used between each element in the publication statement?

A colon is used between the place name and the publisher name. A comma is used between the publisher's name and the publication date.

2. Which of the following use correct ISBD punctuation?

    a. The Oxford companion to music, by Percy A. Scholes.

    b. xliii, 1189 pages, 185 pages of plates : illustrations ; 24 cm.

    c. The Oxford companion to music / by Percy A. Scholes.

    d. The Oxford companion to music : by Percy A. Scholes.

    e. xliii, 1189 pages; 185 pages of plates. Illustrations, 24 cm.

3. *Add ISBD punctuation to the following:*
   a. Morocco modern / Herbert Ypma.
   b. New York : Thames & Hudson, 2010.
   c. 157 pages : color illustrations, 22 cm.
   d. The red and the blacklist : the intimate memoir of a Hollywood expatriate / Norma Barzman.
   e. New York : Thunder's Mouth Press, 2003.
   f. xi, 464 pages, 8 unnumbered pages of plates : portraits, 24 cm.

EXERCISE 2.3

1.   a. *By what name(s) is this work known that might be searched by a library patron?*
     This work is known by the title: Saved by cake.
     b. *What format is it? How can you tell?*
     This is a book, it has pages and illustrations.
     c. *What names are associated with this work? What are the role(s) of people named?*
     Marian Keyes wrote the book, she is the author.
     Alistair Richardson's photographs are included, he is the photographer.
     d. *What is the work about? How can you tell?*
     The work is about Marian Keyes' mental health, and depression. The subject headings used to describe the work tell you what the book is about.
     e. *What numbers are associated with this work?*
     There are 2 ISBNs: 9780718158897 and 071815889X (ISBN stands for International Standard Book Number) and an OCLC number: 759584428.

2.   a. *By what name(s) is this work known that might be searched by a library patron?*
     This work is known by 2 titles: Soccer unites the world and The Beautiful game.
     b. *What format is it? How can you tell?*
     The format is a map on a sheet of paper. The description provides details of the format.
     c. *What is the scale and projection method?*
     The scale is 1:78,630,000 or 1 inch equals 1,241 miles. The projection method is Winkel Tripel projection.
     d. *What names are associated with this work?*
     There are 2 names are associated with this work:
     National Geographic Maps and National Geographic Society.

3.   a. *By what name(s) is this work known that might be searched by a library patron?*
     This work is known by the title: Chansons d'amour Edith Piaf.
     b. *What format is it? How can you tell?*
     The format is a CD on a 12 cm disc. The description provides details of the format.
     c. *What is the role of Edith Piaf?*
     Edith Piaf is the singer. This is explained in the creator field.
     d. *What information is given in the contents field?*
     The contents field provides a list of all the songs included on the CD.

EXERCISE 3.1

Highlight all the access points you might expect in these catalog records.

1. AUTHOR   Lang, Kenneth R.
   TITLE   The Cambridge guide to the solar system / Kenneth R. Lang.
   SUBJECT   1) Solar system.
             2) Astronomy.

2. TITLE: 2014 FIFA World Cup Brazil.
   ALSO TITLED: FIFA World Cup Brazil
                       Brazil
   SUBJECTS: World Cup (Soccer) (2014 : Brazil)
                       Fédération internationale de football association -- Computer games.
                       Soccer -- Computer games.
                       Xbox video games.
                       Video games.
   OTHER AUTHORS: EA Sports (Firm)
                       Fédération internationale de football association

EXERCISE 3.2

1 a. Which is the authorized access point?
Menzies, Robert, Sir, 1894-1978

EXERCISE 3.3

1 a. Which are the authorized access points to be used for this person in the catalog?
Rowling, J. K.
Galbraith, Robert
b. What will happen if a client looks up 'Rowling, Jo'?
The catalog identifies the other headings that could be used for this author and refers the client to the authorized access points - Rowling, J. K. and Galbraith, Robert
c. Do all these entries refer to the same person?
Yes, the entries all refer to the same person as this author has written under a number of pseudonyms.

2 a. Which is the authorized access point to be used for this organization in the catalog?
Canada. Atmospheric Environment Service
b. What does the 'see also' reference mean?
This organization was previously known as Canada. Meteorological Branch but the name was changed so only resources published since the name change will be found with 'Canada. Atmospheric Environment Service' as the authorized access point. Resources published prior to the name change will be cataloged using the previous authorized access point 'Canada. Meteorological Branch'.
c. Might a catalog contain more than one of these access points? Under what circumstances?
Yes, a catalog might contain more than one of these access points if the library holds resources that were published when the name of the organization was different. Publications are cataloged using the name of the organization that was current at the time of publication.

EXERCISE 3.4

1. a. What type of material is this?
This is a book.
b. *What is the title?*
The title is 'Waste : a philosophy of things'.
c. *Who is the author?*
The author of this book is William Viney.
d. *Is it illustrated?*
Yes the book is illustrated.

e. *Write down the ISBN.*
The ISBN is 9781472527578 (hbk.)
f. *What is this publication about?*
This publication is about refuse (commonly known as garbage) and refuse disposal in literature, in art and the philosophy of refuse and refuse disposal. It also discusses the philosophy of antiquities, ruins in literature, and the economics of waste in literature.

2. a. *What type of material is this?*
This resource is a map.
b. *What is the title?*
The title is 'Seattle, Washington'.
c. *Is it colored or black and white?*
The map is colored.
d. *Who produced it?*
The map was produced by AAA (Organization : U.S.).
e. *Is it part of a series? If so, what is the name of the series?*
It is part of the 'City series'.
f. *What is it about?*
This resource is a map of the Seattle Metropolitan Area.

EXERCISE 3.5

1. a. *What type of material is described in this catalog entry?*
This catalog entry describes a monograph.
b. *Who is the author?*
The author of the resource is Nicholas Cox.
c. *Who printed this item?*
The resource was printed by Freeman Collins for Nicholas Cox.
d. *What is the date of publication?*
The date of publication was 1686.
e. *Which edition is this publication?*
This publication is the 3rd ed.
f. *Is it illustrated?*
Yes the resource is illustrated.
g. *Does it include an index?*
No it does not include an index.
h. *What is this publication about?*
This publication is about fowling, hunting, falconry, fishing, forestry law and legislation in Great Britain and game laws in Great Britain.
i. *How could you find other books on this subject?*
You could find other books on this subject by looking to see what else is listed in the catalog under these subject headings. Depending on the ILS you may be able to navigate directly from the subject headings in this catalog record. It would also be worthwhile looking on the shelves at the same classification number to see if there are other resources shelved with this one.
j. *Which classification scheme does this library use?*
This library uses the Dewey Decimal Classification.
k. *Why do you think this publication cannot be borrowed?*
As this item is very old it may be rare or fragile so it cannot be borrowed.

2. a. *What type of material is described in this catalog entry?*
This resource is a DVD.

b. Who is the creator?
It was created by Ken Loach, who was the film producer.
c. Who is the publisher of this item?
The publisher of this resource is Dogwoof.
d. What is it about?
This resource focuses on Great Britain in 1945. It discusses social change, public welfare, the coal strike in Great Britain in 1984-1985. It also considers the political situation and the social conditions at that time.
e. What is the playing time?
512 minutes

3. *a. What type of material is described in this catalog entry?*
   This resource is a periodical.
   b. When was the first issue of this publication published?
   The first issue was published in 1969.
   c. In what language is it published?
   It is published in English, French and Spanish, with each translation containing summaries in the other two languages.
   d. How would you find other items on the same topic/s?
   You could find other resources on this subject by looking to see what else is listed in the catalog under the subject headings. Depending on the ILS you may be able to navigate directly from the subject headings in this catalog record. It would also be worthwhile looking on the shelves at the same classification number to see if there are other resources shelved with this one.

EXERCISE 4.1

1. *How does the CIP Program work?*
   The Cataloging in Publication (CIP) Program is a free service offered to publishers by national libraries to provide a catalog record for new and forthcoming publications in advance of their publications. The library creates a bibliographic record for each publication and sends it to the publisher. The publisher prints the record (known as CIP data) on the verso of the title page. For each library that acquires a copy of the book, the CIP data is available to use for their catalog record.

2. *What is the purpose of the CIP Program?*
   The purpose of the CIP Program is to serve the nation's libraries by cataloging books in advance of publication. The CIP entry is added to the national database, which provides libraries, booksellers and the general public with advance notice of forthcoming publications. The database is shared with international library networks and also exposed to search engines such as Google. The CIP alerts the library community to forthcoming publications and facilitates acquisition of new resources.

3. *Who is eligible for the CIP Program?*
   The Cataloging in Publication (CIP) program covers new and revised editions of works published within the country. To be eligible for the program, publications should be:
   a. published in that country
   b. relevant to a wide audience with substantial textual information content
   c. likely to be acquired and made available by libraries within that country.

EXERCISE 4.2

1a.

```
000  02032cam a2200421 i 4500
008  130710s2015    maua    b    001 0 eng
010  __  $a 2013027707
020  __  $a 9781284036695
040  __  $a DNLM/DLC $c DLC $e rda $d DLC
042  __  $a pcc
050  00  $a TX361.A8 $b .F56 2015
082  00  $a 613.2024796 $2 23
100  1_  $a Fink, Heather Hedrick, $e author.
245  10  $a Practical applications in sports nutrition / $c Heather Hendrick Fink, Alan E. Mikesky.
250  __  $a Fourth Edition.
264  _1  $a Burlington, MA : $b Jones & Bartlett Learning, $c 2015
300  __  $a xxvi, 546 pages : $b illustrations ; $c 28 cm.
336  __  $a text $2 rdacontent
337  __  $a unmediated $2 rdamedia
338  __  $a volume $b nc $2 rdacarrier
504  __  $a Includes bibliographical references and index.
650  12  $a Nutritional Physiological Phenomena.
650  12  $a Sports $x physiology.
650  22  $a Exercise $x physiology.
700  1_  $a Mikesky, Alan E., $e author.
```

1a is the correct record because it describes the fourth edition by Heather Hendrick Fink and Alan Mikesky, published in 2015; whereas record 1b is for the 3rd edition published in 2012 which has three authors.

2b.

```
000  00917cam a22003018i 4500
008  141007s2015    vra        000 0 eng d
020  __  $a 9780670078783 : $c $34.99
040  __  $a ANL $b eng $e rda $d ANL
042  __  $a anuc
082  04  $a 641.5637 $2 23
100  1_  $a Macri, Irena, $e author.
245  10  $a Eat drink Paleo cookbook / $c Irena Macri.
264  _1  $a Melbourne, Vic. : $b Penguin Group (Australia), $c 2015.
300  __  $a 217 pages : $b color illustrations ; $c 25 cm.
336  __  $a text $2 rdacontent
337  __  $a unmediated $2 rdamedia
338  __  $a volume $2 rdacarrier
650  _0  $a High-protein diet $v Recipes.
650  _0  $0 000036126015 $a Reducing diets $v Recipes.
650  _0  $0 000036075118 $a Diet therapy.
650  _0  $a Prehistoric peoples $x Nutrition.
```

2b is the correct record because it describes the book that was published by Penguin Books in Melbourne, Victoria whereas record 2a describes the book published in Great Britain by the author. The correct record also provides full details of the physical characteristics and has more specific subject headings.

3a.

000 02365cam a2200445 a 4500
001 000051862327
003 AuCNLKIN
005 20140903110327.0
008 121008s2013   gw abc   000 0 eng d
020 __ $a 9783791348070
040 __ $a YDXCP $c YDXCP $d BTCTA $d UKMGB $d OCLCQ
050 _4 $a TR99 $b .H66x 2013
082 04 $a 779.095 $2 23
100 1_ $a Hooton, Keiko S.
245 10 $a Contemporary photography in Asia / $c Keiko S. Hooton, Tony Godfrey.
264 _1 $a Munich : $b Prestel, $c 2013.
300 __ $a 223 pages : $b illustrations (chiefly colored), map, ports. ; $c 26 cm.
336 __ $a text $2 rdacontent
337 __ $a unmediated $2 rdamedia
338 __ $a volume $2 rdacarrier
504 __ $a Includes bibliographical references.
650 _0 $a Photography $z Asia.
650 _0 $a Photography, Artistic.
651 _0 $a Asia $v Pictorial works.
700 1_ $a Godfrey, Tony.

3a is the correct record because it provides the first place of publication rather than the last place of publication that is described in the incorrect record. The correct record provides subject headings whereas the incorrect record does not include any subject headings.

EXERCISE 4.3

1. Author: Coombes, Allen J.
   Title: The A to Z of plant names : a quick reference guide to 4000 garden plants / Allen J. Coombs.
   Edition: 1st ed.
   Published: Portland, Or. : Timber Press, c2012.
   Description: 312 pages; 22 cm.
   ISBN: 9781604691962
   Notes: Includes bibliographical references (p. 341-342)
   Subjects: Plants -- Great Britain -- Nomenclature -- Dictionaries.
                   Plants -- North America -- Nomenclature -- Dictionaries.
                   Botany -- Great Britain -- Dictionaries.
                   Botany -- North America -- Dictionaries.

The author's name is spelled 2 different ways in this record. Check the resource and search online for information about this author to determine which form of the name should be used. In the notes field the bibliography is on pages numbered higher than the number of pages in the book. Check the resource to see if this is correct.

The correct record would be:
Author: Coombes, Allen J.
Title: The A to Z of plant names : a quick reference guide to 4000 garden plants / Allen J. Coombes.

Edition:	1st ed.
Published:	Portland, Or. : Timber Press, c2012.
Description:	312 pages; 22 cm.
ISBN:	9781604691962
Notes:	Includes bibliographical references (p. 311-312)
Subjects:	Plants -- Great Britain -- Nomenclature -- Dictionaries.
	Plants -- North America -- Nomenclature -- Dictionaries.
	Botany -- Great Britain -- Dictionaries.
	Botany -- North America -- Dictionaries.

2.

Author:	Hay, Sam, (author).
Title:	Undead pets : Rise of the zombie rabbit and Flight of the battered budgie / by Sam Hay ; read by Toby Longworth.
Also titled:	Rise of the zimbie rabbit
	Flight of the battered birdie
Content type:	text.
Carrier type:	volume.
Edition:	Complete & unabridged.
Published:	Bath, England : AudioGO, 2013.
Description:	pages: CD audio, digital ; 12 cm.
ISBN:	9781471362590
Series:	Chivers CD children's audio books
Contents:	Rise of the zombie rabbit -- Flight of the battered budgie.
Performer:	Reader : Toby Longworth.
Subjects:	Talking books for children.
	Rabbits -- Juvenile fiction.
	Dogs -- Juvenile fiction.
	Budgerigar -- Juvenile.
	Zombies -- Juvenile fiction.
Other authors:	Longworth, Terry, (narrator).

The Also titled fields do not match what is in the Contents field. Typographic errors like this hinder proper indexing and can be frustrating for both staff and library users.

As this is a CD audio book, the extent in the description field should show how many CDs not how many pages are in this resource. The correct description would be:

2 audio discs (2 hr., 10 min.) : CD audio, digital ; 12 cm.

In the Other authors field the narrator's first name is incorrect. His first name is Toby.

The correct record would be:

Author:	Hay, Sam, (author).
Title:	Undead pets : Rise of the zombie rabbit and Flight of the battered budgie / by Sam Hay ; read by Toby Longworth.
Also titled:	Rise of the zombie rabbit
	Flight of the battered budgie
Content type:	text.
Carrier type:	volume.
Edition:	Complete & unabridged.
Published:	Bath, England : AudioGO, 2013.
Description:	2 audio discs (2 hr., 10 min.) : CD audio, digital ; 12 cm.
ISBN:	9781471362590
Series:	Chivers CD children's audio books

Contents:	Rise of the zombie rabbit -- Flight of the battered budgie.
Performer:	Reader : Toby Longworth.
Subjects:	Talking books for children.
	Rabbits -- Juvenile fiction.
	Dogs -- Juvenile fiction.
	Budgerigar -- Juvenile.
	Zombies -- Juvenile fiction.
Other authors:	Longworth, Toby, (narrator).

3. Author: Lahti, Arto.
    Title: Globallization and Afican economics / Arto Lahti.
    Content type: text.
    Carrier type: volume.
    ISBN: 9789526041834 (pbk.)
       9789526041841 (pdf)
    LC call number: HF1611
    Series: Business + economy
    Notes: Includes bibliographical references.
    Subjects: Globalization -- Africa.
       Africa -- Foreign economic relations.
       Africa -- Economic conditions.

The title field has been incorrectly transcribed. Make sure that you transcribe the title as it is written on the resource.
The publication field is missing from the bibliographic record.
     Published: [Helsinki]: Aalto University, [2011]
The description field is missing from the bibliographic record.
     Description: 93 pages; 30 cm.

The correct record would be:
Author: Lahti, Arto.
Title: Globalization and African economics / Arto Lahti.
Content type: text.
Carrier type: volume.
Published: [Helsinki]: Aalto University, [2011]
Description: 93 pages; 30 cm.
ISBN: 9789526041834 (pbk.)
     9789526041841 (pdf)
LC call number: HF1611
Series: Business + economy
Notes: Includes bibliographical references.
Subjects: Globalization -- Africa.
     Africa -- Foreign economic relations.
     Africa -- Economic conditions.

REVISION QUIZ 4.4

1. *What is the difference between original cataloging and copy cataloging?*
   Original cataloging is the process of creating new bibliographic records (in a standardized way, to enable sharing), using appropriate cataloging tools—RDA Toolkit, DDC or LCC, LSCH, etc.

Copy cataloging is the process of cataloging resources using already exisiting bibliographic records and editing it, when necessary, (checking the record using cataloging tools).

Original cataloging places a heavier demand on staff time and takes longer than copy cataloging, so materials are not ready for patrons to use as quickly.

2. *List three ways of obtaining records for copy cataloging.*

   There are several ways that copy cataloging records can be obtained, including:
   i.   manual copy cataloging by finding a record in another catalog or using Cataloging-in-Publication (CIP) records. Once found, these records can either be downloaded, or copied and pasted into your library's catalog
   ii. catalog subscription services that find or create records and sell them to libraries. These services are provided on a commercial basis, offering original and copy cataloging
   iii. purchasing MARC records when you purchase resources from suppliers
   iv. copying a record from a network or consortium that your library belongs to, like OCLC or Libraries Australia
   v.   'triggering' an automatic download by adding your holdings to a record.

3. *List tasks library technicians may perform in a cataloging department.*

   Library technicians may perform the following tasks in locating records for copy cataloging:
   a. verify new headings
   b. copy catalog
   c. enter data onto the system
   d. check and update new headings
   e. maintain authority file
   f. final processing

4. *List the basic steps followed when copy cataloging.*

   The basic steps when cataloging are as follows:
   1. Search the library's catalog for a bibliographic record that matches the item to be cataloged.
      a. Search standard numbers (e.g., ISBN/ISSN/Control number), or
      b. Search title (if no record was found with the standard number search)
   2. If a catalog record is found:
      a. check that the copy cataloging record and the item in hand are the same
         i.   same title and author
         ii. same date of publication and/or edition
         iii. same record control number (eg LC number from CIP, or ISBN/ISSN)
      b. If all these fields match
         i.   Check the correctness of the copy for:
              o descriptive cataloging
              o classification number
              o subject headings
         ii. Accept the copy; or modify it to suit the needs of your library
         iii. Attach holdings information for the new resource.
   3. If no record is found, search another source such as a union catalog (like OCLC, WorldCat, Library of Congress), using the same process as in Steps 1 and 2 above.
   4. If a record is not found in any catalog, set the resource aside for original cataloging.

ACTIVITY 4.5

Your answers may differ from these, as libraries vary significantly.

ACTIVITIES	Librarian	Library Technician	Clerical Assistant	P/T Help
1. Establishes policies and procedures				
2. Supervision			( )	
3. Does original cataloging		( )		
4. Performs bibliographic checking for access points				
5. Solves difficult bibliographic checking problems				
6. Catalogs material with cataloging information available				
7. Locates records in catalogs				
8. Does descriptive and subject cataloging on problem material		( )		
9. Checks cataloging				
10. Catalogs by comparing with existing catalog records				
11. Checks cataloging using existing catalog records				
12. Checks entry of cataloging data				
13. Prepares books for circulation				
14. Supervises book preparation				
15. Maintains authority files				

EXERCISE 5.1

Answers might include

Type of library	Client group
Public library	General public living or working in a particular local government area including children, adults, senior citizens, and special groups such as housebound, physically disabled, visually impaired. Public from out of the area upon payment of a deposit or fee.
School or college library	Teaching staff, administrative staff, students, parents, or occasionally staff from similar institutions. Public upon payment of a deposit or fee.
National library	Staff, other libraries, scholars and researchers, and the public.
Special library	Employees (may be divided into different categories of employees). Employees from related or cooperating organizations, contractors upon payment of a fee or deposit.

ACTIVITY 5.3

Verify the registration policies of different libraries in your area.

Answers might include

Type of library	Proof of identification
School library	Students: name on class list, student card Teachers: pay slip, name on staff list
College library	Students: student card, instructor's letter, fee receipt Staff: pay slip or staff identification card Staff from similar institutions: pay slip, letter of introduction, student card
Special library	Security identification, pay slip, supervisor's authority

REVISION QUIZ 5.8

1. Why do libraries distinguish among different categories of borrowers?

Libraries distinguish among different categories of borrowers in order to provide different services for clients based on their needs.

2. When do libraries keep the registration card that is filled in by the borrower?

Libraries keep the registration card that is filled in by the borrower when there is a need to keep a signature showing agreement to library policies, particularly the conditions of borrowing.

3. What is a 'hold'? Choose the correct answer.

a. The library agrees to keep a book from the shelves until the client picks it up.

b. The library keeps a book for another client when it is returned from loan.

c.. A client requests a book that is on order in the catalog be held for him.

d. The library puts a book into a special collection because it is in demand and only lends it for a short period.

4. Why is the attitude of circulation staff toward clients so important?

The attitude of circulation staff toward clients is so important because the circulation desk is usually the first point of contact and people may judge all library services on the quality of service they experience there.

5. When checking out material, you are often given the choice of printing a receipt for all the items loaned out. What is the purpose of this slip?

The purpose of printing a receipt for items loaned out is to show when items are due back in the library.

6. Under what circumstances would a library consider re-barcoding some or all of the collection?

A library could consider re-barcoding some or all of the collection to make it possible to introduce self-checkout stations into the library.

7. When would a borrower ask for a renewal?

A borrower will ask for a renewal when they require the item beyond the date it is due.

8. Why do libraries fine clients for having items overdue?
Libraries fine clients for having items overdue to encourage people to return library materials by the due date. This helps to make the materials available for other library clients to use.

EXERCISE 5.9
Consider a library where you are familiar with the short loan or reserve section.
1. List the issues for library staff in managing such a collection.
Issues for library staff who manage a short loan or reserve section may include:
- the need for extra space to keep the materials in a secure area and prevent unauthorized use
- the need for extra staffing to retrieve materials for students and to book items
- extra marking of items to identify their status more easily
- rudeness and distress of clients who are unable to access an item when needed, especially just before assignments are due
- communication with teachers so that material is put into the reserve collection when students need it
- ensuring that teachers review the collection regularly so that only required material is kept on reserve
- students might rely only on material put aside for them rather than using the whole collection.

2. List the issues for library clients in using such a collection.
Issues for clients include:
- heavy fines and penalties discouraging use
- high demand for some materials and limited loan periods restricting use
- an in-library-only use policy disadvantaging part-time and distance education students
- the need to plan ahead rather than waiting until deadlines are imminent.

REVISION QUIZ 5.10
1. Why do libraries set up special short loan or reserve sections?
Libraries set up special short loan or reserve sections when a large number of library users need access to materials, usually for a short time.

2. Name three differences between short loan conditions and normal loan conditions.
Short loans are usually a few hours or one night, materials are shelved in a secure area and incur heavier fines and penalties if not returned on time.
Normal loan periods are often 2-3 weeks, collections are open to library patrons for browsing and late returns incur nominal fines.

3. Where do the materials on reserve come from?
The materials on reserve might come from the library's collection, an instructor's personal copy of a book or lecture notes, or photocopies temporarily made available.

4. What types of libraries use a reserve system?
Academic libraries, school and special libraries might use a reserve system.

EXERCISE 6.3

1. *Find the title of a book by Nadine Gordimer.*
   There are many books by Nadine Gordimer, including: *A world of strangers, Occasion for loving, Get a life, Living in hope and history, The conservationist, Burger's daughter* and *July's people, The lying days, A guest of honour, A sport of nature, My son's story.*

2. *Find the title of a book about Nadine Gordimer.*
   Books about Nadine Gordimer include: *Betrayals of the body politic: the literary commitments of Nadine Gordimer* by Andrew V. Ettin; *Nadine Gordimer's Burger's daughter : a casebook* by Judie Newman; *The novels of Nadine Gordimer : history from the inside* by Stephen Clingman.

3. *Give the author and title of a book by Haruki Murakami.*
   Books by Haruki Murakami include: *Kafka on the shore, Norwegian wood, The wind-up bird chronicle, A wild sheep chase, 1Q84, Colorless Tsukuru Tazaki and his years of pilgrimage.*

4. *Who wrote a criticism in English of Margaret Atwood's book 'The handmaid's tale'? What is the title?*
   The following are criticisms of Margaret Atwood's *The handmaid's tale*: Wilson, Sharon Rose, Freidman, Thomas B., Hengen, Shannon, *Approaches to teaching Atwood's The handmaid's tale and other works*; Foster, Malcolm, *Margaret Atwood's The handmaid's tale*; Michael, Magali Cornier, *Feminism and the postmodern impulse: post-World War II fiction*; Thompson, Lee Briscoe, *Scarlet letters: Margaret Atwood's The handmaid's tale.*

5. *To which series does Mary Jane DeMarr's book about Barbara Kingsolver belong?*
   Critical companions to popular contemporary writers

6. *Find Thea Hayes' memoir about her life as a nurse. Transcribe the title and statement of responsibility.*
   An outback nurse by Thea Hayes.

7. *When was Nelson Mandela born? When did he die?*
   Mandela, Nelson, 1918-2013

8. *What is the full title information for the book with ISBN 9780061733123*
   The title is *Digital barbarism : a writer's manifesto*

9. *Find a Braille version of 'Cloudy with a chance of meatballs'. Who is the author? Who produced the Braille version?*
   Cloudy with a chance of meatballs, Braille version is by Judi Barrett. It is published by National Braille Press.

EXERCISE 6.4 (OPTIONAL)

If you receive ILL requests for these items, decide whether they meet the criteria of the Copyright Act in your country. Which of them require declarations?

1. *Kowalski, Suzanne, 'Rhythm, roles and responsibility: the Steiner philosophy explored', 'Bedrock', Vol. 2, issue 4*
   and
   Low, Carol and Anh Nguyen, 'Suffer the little children: understanding the needs of child refugees', 'Bedrock', Vol. 2, issue 4

Is it a single copy for client's personal use or for inclusion in the library collection? - We can assume this if it is for 1 copy.

Is it a reasonable portion? - No. The request is for more than 1 article in a single issue, but they are not on the same subject.

Is it available for purchase in a reasonable time and at a reasonable cost? - This would have to be investigated. For ILL you may assume that the requesting library has investigated and found that it is not available.

The client must make a declaration regarding use. The library must declare that it is satisfied that the item is unavailable for purchase.

2. *The chapter about Ra, the god of radiance (pages 11- 24) in Donna Jo Napoli's book, 'Treasury of Egyptian mythology : classic stories of gods, goddesses, monsters & mortals' that was published in Washington, D.C. by National Geographic in 2013. The book has 192 pages.*

Is it a single copy for the client's personal use or for inclusion in library collection? - We can assume this if it is for 1 copy.

Is it a reasonable portion? - Yes.

You may copy.

Library must make a declaration regarding use.

3. *Pages 83-128 of 'Greenvoe' by George Mackay Brown (London, Penguin, 1972) to replace missing pages in the library's copy. It is a 249 page book.*

Is it a single copy for client's personal use or for inclusion in library collection? - We can assume this if it is for 1 copy.

Is it a reasonable portion? - It is more than 10% and will only be considered a reasonable portion if it is all in one chapter. If it is in one chapter you may copy.

Is it available for purchase in a reasonable time and at a reasonable cost? - This would have to be investigated. For ILL you may assume that the requesting library has investigated and found that it is not available.

Client must make a declaration regarding use. The library must make a declaration that it is satisfied that the material is unavailable for purchase.

4. *The whole of 'An outline Of European architecture' by Nikolaus Pevsner. It was published in 1983, has been out of print for 25 years and is rarely seen by secondhand booksellers.*

Is it a single copy for client's personal use or for inclusion in library collection? - We can assume this if it is for 1 copy.

Is it a reasonable portion? - It is more than 10% and will only be considered a reasonable portion if it is all in one chapter. If it is in one chapter you may copy.

Is it available for purchase in a reasonable time and at a reasonable cost? – No it is not available for purchase as it is out of print. You may copy

Client must make a declaration regarding use. The library must make a declaration that it is satisfied that the material is unavailable for purchase.

REVISION QUIZ 6.6

1. *Name two ways in which libraries receive ILL requests from other libraries.*

Libraries receive interlibrary loan requests from other libraries: electronically via ILL networks such as OCLC, LADD; by email; by fax; or occasionally by phone.

2. *Name three types of material that libraries prefer not to lend.*

Items that may not be available for interlibrary loan could include:

- reference material

- short loan collection
- audio-visual material
- textbooks
- bound journals
- items in special or rare book collections
- manuscript material
- genealogy books
- dissertations
- theses.

3. *What methods do libraries use to send items loaned through ILL?*
   Libraries could send resources loaned through ILL in one of the following ways:
   - email
   - file transfer
   - fax
   - courier
   - postal delivery
   - express post
   - borrower collecting from supplier

4. *Under what circumstances are libraries permitted to copy material for another library?*
   Libraries are able to copy print material for another library if:
   - it is a single copy for a user of the requesting library, or for inclusion in the collection of the requesting library (not a second copy - unless the first copy was lost), AND
   - it is a reasonable portion of a work, OR
   - if not a reasonable portion, the officer in charge of the requesting library must be satisfied that it is not available for purchase in a reasonable time and at a reasonable cost. The officer in charge must sign a statutory declaration to this effect.

ACTIVITY 7.1
Answer the following questions about acquisitions.
2. *What are approval plans? Find a description of one on a library book vendor's website.*
   Approval plans are agreements with a vendor to regularly deliver all recent publications that meet certain criteria (called an approval profile) based on the amount of money allocated to the approval plan.

EXERCISE 7.2
1. *Are there any differences between the resources received, the invoice and the order records?*
   The oil man and the sea
   The title ordered is: *The oil man and the sea: navigating the northern gateway.*
   You received a version with a different subtitle (*A modern misadventure on the Pacific tanker route*) and the same ISBN. Occasionally resources are given different titles by the publisher in order to market to different countries.
   The Hobbit
   You received the October 2011 edition, ISBN-13: 9780261103344 which is a paperback version. The order placed was for the *The Hobbit* 70th Anniversary Edition, also paperback, ISBN-13: 9780261103283
   If the anniversary edition includes features that the requestor really wants, you may have to return it and explain to the vendor that you require the anniversary edition.

Sport as a business

Sport as a business is OK but in the order record, the form field says ebook. Is the format coded correctly in the record? It may be a good idea to confirm with the requestor which format is preferred.

Australian gardens

Australia gardens is OK.

2. *Did you notice any notes that require further attention?*
   There is a hold on the *Sport as a business* book.

3. *Are there any errors in the order records?*
   There is one error : in the order record the author's name is misspelled, Aitkens should be Aitken.

Exercise 7.4

1. *What is the full title of a serial called 'Women & literature'? What is the ISSN?*
   Serial title is *Women & literature : a journal of women writers and the literary treatment of women* and the ISSN is 0147-1759.

2. *What is the title of the serial with ISSN 0949-149X? Is it still being published?*
   ISSN 0949-149X is *The International journal of engineering education*, which began in 1992 and is still being published.

3. *When was the first issue of 'Chemical abstracts' published?*
   The first issue of *Chemical abstracts* was published in January 1907.

4. *'The journal of supply change management' (published by the National Association of Purchasing Management) has changed its title several times. Give one of its former titles with ISSN.*
   International journal of purchasing and materials management (ISSN 1055-6001)
   Journal of purchasing and materials management (ISSN 0094-8594)
   Journal of purchasing (ISSN 0022-4030)

5. *'Rolling Stone' is American but is there also an Australian edition? If so, do any American libraries have a subscription to it?*
   Yes there is also an Australian edition of *Rolling Stone* published in Sydney. Worldcat.org has a search feature to enter your postal code and it will locate a library near you that has subscription.

Revision Quiz 8.7

1. *Why is it important to maintain the physical objects in a collection?*
   It is important to maintain a library's collection because:
   - Library materials are often expensive or impossible to replace
   - Materials should be kept in good condition and order to make sure that they are accessible and ready to use
   - Users are more inclined to use materials that are in good condition and tend to avoid shabby or damaged material.

2. *What is a spine label?*
   A spine label is a label that is affixed to the spine of library materials to show the call number and location details for an item.

3. *Why do libraries cover books?*
   Libraries cover books to strengthen them and to protect them from damage and soiling.

4. *What is meant by final processing?*
   Final processing is the physical preparation of library materials for inclusion in the collection. It may involve covering or strengthening them or protecting them by placement in boxes or folders.

5. *Name three factors that will affect the storage methods chosen by a library.*
   Factors that affect the storage methods chosen by a library include:
   - cost
   - appearance
   - the space available
   - the library's clientele
   - the need to prevent damage to materials
   - staffing levels
   - the rarity of the materials
   - the special needs of specific formats.

EXERCISE 9.1

1. F ARC	2. F GRI	3. F KOC (Highways)	4. F KOC (Year)	5. F MCC
6. F RUS	7. F THE (Happy)	8. F THE (My other)	9. F TRO (Men)	10. F TRO (Next)

EXERCISE 9.2

1.

1. 004.1 COM	2. 025.1 ORG	3. 158.2 BOD	4. 302.2 COM	5. 331.12 LIF
6. 380.1 MAR	7. 428 FRO	8. 495.6 MEE	9. 519.5 AGA	10. 551.6 HOL
11. 617.8 UND	12. 640.42 YOU	13. 796.46 ATL	14. 808.02 ESS	15. 822.3 CRE
16. 882.01 ANT	17. 914 GRE	18. 940.28 IND	19. 944 LAN	20. 959.86 DON

2.

1. 510 NGU	2. 510.76 BRO	3. 512.5 IFR	4. 513.93 ORD	5. 515.1 HAE
6. 519.5 MAS	7. 531.6 SPU	8. 551.8 BUT	9. 573.2 LEA	10. 574.13 VAN
11. 591 SMI	12. 591.68 HOW	13. 914.59 PIL	14. 915.4 JOH	15. 919.5 MAC
16. 935.01 LAN	17. 949.3 HAE	18. 952.01 ISH	19. 994.05 BOL	20. 994.51 EAS

EXERCISE 9.3

1. 001.64 STA	2. 001.6404 OGD	3. 001.64404 CHO	4. 005.26 BAS	5. 005.262 TUR
6. 020.6224205 LIB	7. 020.941 LIB	8. 052.94 AUS	9. 158.05 JOU	10. VIDEO 332.6324 AUS
11. 333.330688 CAN	12. 333.3387 SUC	13. SERIAL 346.9407 BUS	14. 614.0994 AUS	15. REF 614.59623 KIL
16. VIDEO 641.5676 LON	17. 949.5 MEN	18. REF 949.5074 GAG	19. SERIAL 994.020924 WAR	20. REF 994.03 CLU

EXERCISE 9.4

1. REF 001.640321 ABR	2. REF 328.73 AUS	3. REF 791.45 CON	4. 011.38 HOP	5. 011.6403 NEV
6. 016.31 STA	7. 016.35471 IND	8. 016.35494093 GAR	9. SERIAL 021.0025 INT	10. 021.002541 BRI
11. 328.73 CON	12. 341.2 TRI	13. 378.33 GRA	14. 378.43 BAR	15. 520.321 ENG
16. SERIAL 590.744 INT	17. 705.8 AME	18. VIDEO 020.321 HIL	19. VIDEO 314.2 WHI	20. VIDEO 509.22 DON

EXERCISE 9.5

1.	2.	3.	4.	5.
346.991 W587	360 Y92	363.25 G255	363.25 G256	363.25 L131
6.	7.	8.	9.	10.
363.25 M475	364 B112	364 H229	364.021 D562	364.099 A477
11.	12.	13.	14.	15.
364.0994 C929	364.49 C928	364.49 C929	364.49 M476	364.994 A198
16.	17.	18.	19.	20.
364.994 C297	364.99402 C444	364.994021 M953	364.994021 W181	364.994021 W182

EXERCISE 9.6

1.

1.	2.	3.	4.	5.
GN	GN	GN	GN	GN
324	325	325	326	326
.F531	.F47	.F7	.F5	.F5
1986		1979	1989	1991

2.

1.	2.	3.	4.	5.
Z699	Z699.5	Z699.5	Z699.5	Z699.5
.B53	.B5	.B53	.B53	.B53
.D3	.D37	.D3	.D37	.D37
1986	1985	1984	1983	1987

3.

1.	2.	3.	4.	5.
PL42	PL282	PL2842	PL2892	PL8224
.A552	.A5	.A2	.A52	.A502
.M606	.M7	.M61	.M6	.M76
1993	1942		1987	1990

4.

1.	2.	3.	4.	5.
BF575 .S75K44	BF575 .9 .A86	GT4985 .N38	HJ2193 .F56	HJ2193 .S97
6.	7.	8.	9.	10.
HJ9931 .A44	HN850 .V5A97	HN850 .Z9V58	HV1 .C74	JA26 .A86
11.	12.	13.	14.	15.
JQ4011 .E49	Q1 .S34	QB1 .A89441	QB1 .R47	QB1 .5 .M67

16. QB51 .A77	17. QB86 .S35	18. QL737 .C23T475	19. TX717 .P43	20. TX724 .5 .B47

5.

1. DG5 .I61	2. DU967 .6 .K29	3. HM1 .A5	4. HM1 .A87	5. HM1 .5 .C72
6. HN850 .V5A97	7. HN850 .Z9V53	8. HN850 .Z9V58	9. HQ1101 .W74	10. HV1 .C74
11. JA26 .A86	12. Q1 .R553	13. Q1 .R56	14. QB1 .5 .M67	15. QH540 .B75
16. QH540 .C3	17. QH540 .C38	18. QH540 .C4	19. SD1 .7 .W4	20. T1 .226 .U54

6.

1. DS611 .I44	2. HA31 .2 .M66	3. HD5345 .A6 .C74	4. HT609 R43	5. HT609 .R5
6. HT609 .S33	7. HV9069 .C53	8. JV9185 .I8 .C72	9. NC1115 .B7	10. PA2117 .A5
11. QA276 .8 .H34	12. QH508 .B3	13. QH508 .G7	14. QH511 .H35	15. QP33 .5 .C3
16. QP34 .L348	17. QP171 .S58	18. R127 .2 .V58	19. RC632 .P56 .I57	20. S494 .5 .W3

REVISION QUIZ 9.9

1. *What is a closed access library?*

A closed access library holds a collection which does not allow the library user to collect materials directly from the shelves. Library staff collect materials for the clients.

2. *Why do some libraries choose to shelve their materials in a fixed location?*

Some libraries choose to shelve their materials in a fixed location because:
- space is used more economically
- the collection does not need to be re-spaced as often as with relative location
- there is less wear and tear on resources.

3. *Why do libraries use a classification scheme to organize the materials on their shelves?*
Libraries use a classification scheme because it enables them to organize the materials in subject order on the shelves. This means that users can browse the collection and find related materials sitting on the shelves together.

4. *Why is it important to reshelve items promptly?*
It is important to reshelve materials promptly to avoid unnecessary effort involved in searching for 'missing' items and to avoid causing frustration for users.

5. *Give three OH&S rules you should follow when shelving.*
The OH&S rules you must follow when shelving materials include:
• Use a kick stool to work above shoulder level rather than stretching for a shelf you can barely reach.
• Sit on a kick stool when working below waist level rather than crouching or bending over.
• Pick up books with both hands rather than using one hand.
• Turn around using your feet rather than twisting your body.
• Shelve for not more than 3 hours a day.
• Try to vary tasks while shelving.
• Vary your movements while shelving and pay attention to your body as you move.
• Ensure that book trucks are evenly and not too heavily loaded because they can topple easily.

EXERCISE 10.2
File the following sets of entries word by word, using the 1980 ALA filing rules.
1.
Air and space resources
Air conditioning
Air cushion vehicles
Air Force
Air, Lesley
Air pollution
Air transport
Aircraft
Airfields
Airports

2.
Go down Moses
Go tell it on the mountain
Goannas
Gold and silver
Gold fever
Gold mining
Golden girls
Golf for amateurs
Gondolas of Venose
Gone is gone
Good housekeeping
Good wives
Goodbye cruel world
Goodness gracious me
Goody Townhouse

3.

Engineers unlimited
Engines and trains
England and the near east
Englisch Sprechen!
Englische dogges
English historical documents
English literature
English men of literature
Englishmen
The enigma of drug addiction

4.

A is for alphabet
The Acts
An Approach to Hamlet
Approach to housing
An April After
Archaeology and Old Testament
The Archaeology of Carajou
The Danger of Equality
Danger on the ski trails
Label manufacturing
The labour gang
The labrador puppies
Ladders and snakes
The language laboratory
The laundry basket
Lexicon of jargon
A Lexicon of the German language
That was summer
That's me
That's the way

5.

12 x 8 : Paper read to the Crown Club
$12 to May
20 + 20 = 40
20/- change
20% profit
Twelve angry jelly beans
Twelve drunk teddy bears
Twenty and two
Twenty poems
Twenty soldiers

EXERCISE 10.3
Now file each set letter by letter.

1.
Air and space resources
Air conditioning
Aircraft
Air cushion vehicles
Airfields
Air Force
Air, Lesley
Air pollution
Airports
Air transport

2.
Engineers unlimited
Engines and trains
England and the near east
Englische dogges
Englisch Sprechen!
English historical documents
English literature
Englishmen
English men of literature
Enigma of drug addiction

3.
Goannas
Go down Moses
Gold and silver
Golden girls
Gold fever
Gold mining
Golf for amateurs
Gondolas of Venose
Gone is gone
Goodbye cruel world
Good housekeeping
Goodness gracious me
Good wives
Goody Townhouse
Go tell it on the mountain

EXERCISE 10.4
For each list, decide whether the order is word by word, or letter by letter. State briefly how you recognised the order.
1. The order is letter by letter.
   The terms with the first word 'Cape' are not all filed together.
   The space between Cape and Preston is ignored.

2. The order is word by word.
   The terms with the first word 'File' are all filed together.

3. The order is word by word.
   CD-ROM viewing comes before CD-ROMs.
   Free form comes before FreeCell.

4. The order is letter by letter.
   Spaces are ignored.
   Hawkesbury comes before Hawkes Butchery.

Exercise 10.5

Use the ALA filing rules to arrange each of these bibliographies in correct word by word order.
1.

Baker, Sarah Louise, Bennett, Andy and Taylor, Jodie Louise, *Redefining mainstream popular music*, http//www.routledge.com/books/details/9780415807821/, 2013-06-21.

Cardany, Audrey Berger, 'Music activities for 'Lemonade in Winter'', *General Music Today*, vol. 27, no. 2, January 2014, page 36.

Everett, Walter, E*xpression in pop-rock music*, 2nd ed. New York, Routledge, 2008.

Garofalo, Reebee, *Rockin' out : Popular music in the U.S.A.*, Upper Saddle River, Pearson, 2014.

Hitchins, Ray, *Vibe merchants : the sound creators of Jamaican popular music*, Burlington, VT Ashgate, 2014.

Plasketes, George. *B-Sides, Undercurrents and overtones : peripheries to popular in music, 1960 to the present,* Burlington, Ashgate, 2009.

Rechniewski, Peter, 'The permanent underground: Australian contemporary jazz in the new millennium', *Platform Papers*, No. 16, 2008, pages 1-59.

Spicer, Mark and John Covach, *Sounding out pop : analytical essays in popular music*, Ann Arbor, University of Michigan Press, 2010.

Toft, Robert, *Hits and misses : crafting top 40 singles, 1963-197,*. New York, Continuum, 2010.

Zak, Albin J. III, *I don't sound like nobody : remaking music in 1950s*, Ann Arbor, University of Michigan Press, 2010.

2.

Access: the supplementary index to Internet serials, Washington, DC, Gaylord, 1975-

IEEE and The Open Group. 'Standard for Information Technology—Portable Operating System Interface (POSIX®)', *Base Specifications,* Issue 7, *2013*. Digital file.

IEEE transactions on information technology, New York, Institute of Engineers, 1955.

I.B.M. journal of research and development, New York, International Business Machines Corporation, 54: 2, 2010.

I.T.: journal of information technology, Sydney, Macquarie University, 1995-

IEEE/ACM transactions on networking, New York, Institute of Electrical and Electronics Engineers and the Association for Computing Machinery, 22:3, June 2014.

IEEE annals of the history of computing, Los Alamitos, Calif., IEEE Computer Society, 1979-

IEEE transactions on communications, New York, Institute of Electrical and Electronics Engineers, 62:4, April 2014.

IEEE transactions on computers, New York, Institute of Electrical and Electronics Engineers, 1959-

Information sources in information technology, editor, David Haynes, London, de Gruyter Saur, 2013. Digital file.

EXERCISE 10.6

3rd world report
4 weekly poets
24 hours: ABC FM program
Abridged reader's guide to periodical literature
Book review digest
Booklist
The bulletin
Bulletin of the Centre for Children's Books
C.S.R. quarterly report
CSIRO papers
Defence index
Defense abstracts
Four to fourteen
The horn book magazine
A journal of documentation
The journal of early childhood behaviour
Mount Morgan mining review
Mt Isa Mines ecological quarterly
Queensland agricultural review
Queensland. Department of Education. Annual report
Social science abstracts
Sociofile

EXERCISE 10.7 (OPTIONAL)

These entries are in order. Examine them, and decide the filing principles used.
The filing principles are
• numbers are filed as if spelt out
• initial articles are ignored.

One Australia
150 masterpieces of drawing
150,000 years
114 ways to be your own boss
106 funny things
160 feet down
113 teams of netball players
112 2nd form students
One hundred and two H bombs
100 ideas for the pianist
100,000 jelly beans in a bag
One single minute
1050 jewellery designs
1001 fishing trips
One thousand and one nights
One two buckle my shoe
30 bald heads
'39 to '94: the years of change
3000 elephants in a Mini?
3111 buttons

3001 days to blast off
3001: the year of the future
3010 pieces of paper
3101 feet of rope
Twelve lesson course
12 noon
The Twentieth century
20th century Britain
Twentieth century drama

EXERCISE 11.4

Describe how you think a client might react when given these rules. Can you suggest any improvements?

The client would be intimidated by the number of 'do nots' in the rules. There is also the danger that the library might give the client some ideas on how to cause damage!

To improve these rules it would be better to use more positive comments – e.g., Please handle the books with care.

ACTIVITY 11.5

Prepare a list of guidelines for a new member of the library staff on the correct handling of library materials.

Your guidelines should include comments on handling of material, loading of trolleys or book trucks, correct ways to shelve materials and how to handle material when preparing photocopies.

REVISION QUIZ 11.8

1. *How does a library prevent damage caused by people handling the resources?*
   A library prevents damage caused by people handling the materials by:
   * educating its users and staff in correct handling methods
   * restricting access to more valuable or fragile materials
   * substituting originals with copies.

2. *Describe three features of the ideal environment for preventing damage to library materials.*
   The features of the ideal environment for preventing damage to library materials include:
   * the lighting should be not too bright and not too dark
   * the relative humidity should be around 55%
   * the temperature should be around 21ºC
   * air should circulate throughout the collection
   * it may be necessary to fumigate the library to destroy pests.

3. *Why is it important to repair damaged materials promptly?*
   It is important to repair damaged materials promptly to:
   * avoid further damage
   * ensure materials are returned to the shelves ready for use.

4. *Describe four factors which library staff need to consider when deciding whether an item is worth repairing?*
When deciding whether an item is worth repairing, library staff need to consider the following factors:
- is the item needed immediately by a library user?
- does the library hold other copies of the item?
- is it possible to purchase a replacement?
- can the library afford to buy a replacement?
- is the item still in demand or only used infrequently?
- how serious is the damage?
- does the library have the equipment and supplies needed to repair the damage?
- is the item out of date?
- is the information available in a different format?
- does the item belong to a special collection?
- is the item rare or valuable?

5. *Why do many libraries bind their serials?*
Libraries bind their serials to prolong their life and to keep issues together. Binding ensures that the issues stay in logical order as well as protecting them from damage.

EXERCISE 12.1
Library users can become annoyed if the catalog record states that an item is missing. They argue that there is no point in listing an item if it is not available.
Library staff may feel that the record should stay on the system in case the item is found and returned to the collection. Some library users might find the details of a missing item which is relevant to them and then ask the library to obtain the item on interlibrary loan.

EXERCISE 12.2
1. *Do you agree with weeding all books which have not been borrowed in the last three years? Can you think of any problems associated with implementing this guideline?*
Library staff decide whether a book is out of date by examining the loan record for the book.
If a library decided to weed all books which have not been borrowed in the last 3 years it may discard some items which have been used in the library but not borrowed.

2. *How would the library staff keep up-to-date with changes in the curriculum?*
In order to keep up-to-date with changes in the curriculum library staff need to liaise closely with teaching staff.

3. *How would library staff decide whether a book was heavily used?*
Library staff decide whether a book is heavily used by looking at the loan records and also by examining its appearance.

4. *Why has the library decided to give preference to non-print formats of reference materials?*
The library decided to give preference to non-print formats of reference materials because they take up less space. Also print formats are more likely to be damaged.

5. *Why does the library keep only the most recent edition of reference books in the reference collection?*
   The library keeps only the most recent edition of reference books in the reference collection in order to save space there and to allow users to borrow older editions which are shelved with the main collection.

6. *How would library staff check the physical condition of the audiovisual materials?*
   Library staff check the physical condition of audiovisual materials by examining them closely – e.g., running their fingers along the sprocket holes of films to check for cracks. They might run the audiovisual materials on the appropriate equipment to check for damage.

7. *Why is the media department consulted about the cost-effectiveness of repairing audiovisual materials?*
   The library consults the media department about the cost-effectiveness of repairing audiovisual materials because they would have specialised knowledge on whether the materials can be repaired or whether they should be discarded.

8. *Why does the library check to see whether another library holds a serial before cancelling a title?*
   The library checks to see whether another library holds a serial before cancelling a title to make sure that it is not the only library in an area which has that title. If it is the only library it might decide not to cancel the subscription.

9. *Why does the policy include visual observation as a measure of serial use?*
   The policy includes visual observation as a measure of serial use because some serials are used in the library and are not available for loan, therefore the loan records cannot be used to measure use. Also the physical appearance of the serials might be a determining factor in whether to retain or discard a serial.

REVISION QUIZ 12.3

1. *Why do most libraries decide not to inventory the complete collection at once?*
   Most libraries decide not to inventory the complete collection because of the effort involved and because it is usually necessary to close the library which causes disruption to clients and other libraries.

2. *What is a shelflist?*
   A shelflist is the record of the resources in a library. Items in the shelflist are arranged in the same order as the resources on the shelves. A shelflist may be used as:
   - an aid to collection development, to show the strengths, weaknesses and gaps in the collection
   - an inventory record, for stocktaking
   - a historical and statistical record of the collection.

3. *Why is it important to shelf read the collection before doing an inventory?*
   It is important to shelf read the collection before stocktaking to ensure all of the materials are in correct order. If the materials are out of order staff take much longer conducting the stocktake because they have to stop and reshelve items.

4. *Why do libraries weed their collections?*
   The reasons for weeding a library's collection include:
   - Material is worn out physically.
   - Availability of better materials.
   - The item has not been used or borrowed for a long time.
   - Community needs may have changed, curriculum may have changed.
   - Institutional objectives may have changed therefore changing the library's objectives.
   - Unwanted material can get in the way resulting in crowded, untidy shelves which are awkward to use.
   - The costs of storage are too high.

5. *What types of materials are most likely to be weeded from a collection?*
   Libraries are most likely to weed obsolete materials, superseded publications and duplicate copies of materials. They will also weed unsolicited and unwanted donations and materials which are too badly damaged to be worth repairing.

GLOSSARY

This glossary contains only those terms used in *Learn Basic Library Skills*. For a more comprehensive glossary, see Farkas, Lynn, *LibrarySpeak: a glossary of terms in librarianship and information management.*

academic library A library serving the information needs of the students and staff of a university or similar institution

accession To record the particulars of each item as it is received in a library

accession number The unique number given to an item to record its addition to the library

accession record A record with details of the ordering and receipt of an item in a library

accessions 1. Additions to the library stock. 2. The process of accessioning library materials

access point Any part of a catalog or database record, or entry in a bibliography, that enables a user to find the resource

acid free paper Also durable paper, permanent paper. Paper that is pH neutral, and will last longer than paper with acid content

acquisitions 1.The process of adding to a library's collection by purchase, gift or exchange. 2. The material so added

added entry In AACR2, any entry, other than the main entry and subject entries, that represents the resource in the catalog

aggregator A supplier of electronic journals and/or databases that enables the user to subscribe to a set of titles which are then accessed through the supplier's website

Anglo-American Cataloguing Rules Second edition AACR2. A set of rules for descriptive cataloging adopted by libraries in English-speaking countries. Replaced by RDA (*Resource Description and Access*) in 2010

annual (adj) Published once a year. (n) A serial published once a year

appendix (Plural appendices) Additional material such as statistics, tables etc., attached as a separate item at the end of a resource

approval plan A library's instruction to a publisher or supplier to provide one copy of all publications in a particular category, with the right to return them

area of description In an AACR2 catalog record created using the International Standard Bibliographic Description (ISBD), an area of description constitutes a major section of the bibliographic description, dealing with a particular category (e.g., publication details. ISBD nominates nine areas of description)

article A contribution to a serial written by one or more authors

audiovisual material Non-book materials like audiotapes, compact discs, slides, videotapes

author Also personal author. 1. In AACR2, The person chiefly responsible for the intellectual or artistic content of a work. 2. Author: in RDA, a person, family or corporate body responsible for creating a work that is primarily textual in content, regardless of media type (e.g., printed, electronic or tactile text or spoken word) or of genre (e.g., poems, screenplays, blogs)

authority control The control of access points by establishing and using consistent headings

authority file A collection of authority records containing the preferred forms of headings for names, series and subjects. It can be on cards, microfiche or online

authority record A record of the preferred heading for a person, place, corporate body, series or title, giving information about the preferred heading and non-preferred alternatives, as well as notes about how these were derived

authority work The establishment and maintenance of authority files

authorized access point In RDA, the preferred title or name to be used as an access point in a descriptive catalog record

authorized access point for related entity The RDA term for the concept known in AACR2 cataloging as a 'see also reference', it provides a direction from one heading to another when both are used in cataloging

back issue A non-current issue of a serial

back set A set of non-current issues of a serial

banning Forbidding client privileges such as borrowing, usually until fines are paid

barcode Product identification code that can be read by an electronic barcode scanner. Used to identify, order, sell and manage library items using automated systems

barcode reader/scanner A device used to read a barcode into a computer

bi-annual Issued twice a year

bibliographic Related to books or other library materials

bibliographic control The creation, organization, and management of records to describe resources held in libraries or databases, and to facilitate user access

bibliographic description Description of a resource by title, statement of responsibility, edition, date, publishing information etc.

bibliographic record Also catalog record. A description of a resource in card, microtext, machine-readable or other form containing sufficient information to identify the resource. It may include subject headings and call number

bibliography A list of materials or resources, usually either subject-related or on the works of one author

biennial Issued every two years

binding 1. The type of cover of a book—usually called hardback or paperback, but sometimes cased, hard bound, hard cover (hardback) or limp, softback (paperback). 2. Adding a hard cover to a book or volume of serials

binding record A list of books and/or serials sent to the binder

blanket order An instruction to a publisher or supplier to provide one copy of all publications in a particular category, without the right to return them

blog Online journal, diary or newsletter available on the Web and frequently updated. Shortened form of weblog

blurb Also puff (American usage). Description of a book by the publisher, usually found on the back cover or book jacket, or in an advertising brochure or catalog

book catalog 1. A catalog printed and bound in book format. 2. A substantial list of book titles distributed by a publisher or bookseller

book jobber Also jobber, library supplier. A wholesale bookseller who supplies books to retailers and libraries

book number The numbers, letters or combination of numbers and letters used to distinguish an individual item from other items with the same classification number

borrower Also client. A member of a lending library

branch library A library other than the central library in a system

browse 1. To examine a collection of library materials in an unsystematic way. 2. To look through a list of names, subjects, etc., rather than going straight to a particular term

browser A computer program used to view and interact with the Internet, web servers in private networks, or files in file systems

BT Broader term. A more general subject heading

call number A number on a library item consisting of a classification number, a book number and often a location symbol

caption A heading or title of a chapter, article or page

card catalog A catalog whose 7.5 x 12.5 cm card entries are filed in drawers

catalog A list of library materials contained in a collection, a library or a group of libraries, arranged according to some definite plan

cataloger A person who prepares catalog entries and maintains a catalog so that library materials can be retrieved efficiently

cataloging The preparation of bibliographic information for catalog records. Cataloging consists of descriptive cataloging, subject cataloging and classification

cataloging tools Publications of the international cataloging rules and standards, including *Resource Description and Access, Anglo-American Cataloguing Rules, Library of Congress Subject Headings, Library of Congress Classification, Dewey Decimal Classification*

cessation The termination of publication of a serial

charge code When libraries divide their budget into several accounts for planning purposes, charge codes indicate the account that will be used to pay for the material

charging Recording the loan of an item

check in To record the receipt of (usually a library item returned from loan)

check out To record the loan of (usually a library item being borrowed)

chronological designation Numbering of serials in date order - eg January 2014

circulation Borrowing and returning of library items

circulation desk The area of the library where staff handle loans

circulation list A list of users to whom a publication is to be sent, in the order decided by the library

circulation slip A list of users which is attached to a publication, in the order in which the publication is to be sent

circulation system A system which stores and matches information on a library item, a borrower and the date due

claim A form or letter to a publisher or subscription agent notifying of a serial issue that has not been received

classification A system for arranging library materials according to subject

classification number The number assigned to a library item to indicate a subject and to specify its location in the collection

classification scheme A particular scheme for arranging library materials according to subject (e.g., Dewey Decimal Classification, Library of Congress Classification)

classify To allocate a classification number

client A person who is served by a library or other information agency; also referred to as a borrower, patron, reader, etc.

closed access Where users only have access to items in the collection by requesting them from a member of the library staff. Most often occurs in large research libraries.

closed stack An area containing under-used library materials, only accessible to library staff

collation The physical characteristics of an item, including number of pages, illustrations, size

collection maintenance All the tasks required to maintain the library collection for the use of readers (e.g., shelving, weeding, repair)

Compactus A storage system which consists of shelving units on rails designed to save space

compiler 1. A person who selects and puts together material written by other people 2. A person who writes a reference work made up of many different entries like a dictionary

complete stocktake Checking the contents of the whole collection against the record of the library's holdings

conservation Protecting library and other material from avoidable damage or deterioration without adding to or altering it

continuous stocktake Checking the contents of one section of the library at a time against the record of the library's holdings. It may take several years to stocktake the whole collection

copy cataloging The process of copying cataloging details from an existing catalog record, and adding local location and holdings details

copyright The right given by law to authors, composers or publishers to sell, reproduce or publish a work during a stated period of time

copyright date The date associated with a claim of protection under copyright, identified in a resource by the symbol ©

Cutter number A system of author numbers, devised by Charles A. Cutter, beginning with the first letter of the author's name and followed by numbers. Used in Library of Congress Classification for authors, titles and geographic areas

Cutter-Sanborn number An extension of the Cutter author number system, outlined in the Cutter-Sanborn Threefigure Tables. Designed to maintain works with the same classification number in alphabetical order of author

database A collection of records in machine-readable format, each record being the required information about one item

data element A single piece of information (e.g., date of publication)

date of publication The earliest year in which the particular edition of the work was published (e.g., if a second edition was published in 1991, and reprinted without alteration in 1993, the date of publication of this edition is 1991)

demand driven acquisition DDA. Patron driven acquisition, PDA. An acquisition model applied to buying e-books, in which libraries include entries for possible acquisition in their catalog, and a title is triggered for purchase once a significant number of patrons request it

description Information about a resource derived from the resource itself, including title, statement of responsibility, edition, publication details, physical characteristics, series and ISBN

descriptive cataloging The part of cataloging that describes a resource in terms of its physical (or electronic equivalent) details, and identifies and formulates access points

Dewey Decimal Classification DDC. A classification scheme, devised by Melvil Dewey in 1873, using numbers to represent subjects

digitization The process of converting data into digital format to enable it to be displayed on a computer screen

discharging Cancelling a loan record when an item is returned

distributor An agent which has marketing rights for an item

document delivery The delivery of published and unpublished information by conventional and electronic means, including electronic mail

download To transfer a file from another computer to one's own computer

dust jacket Paper cover for a hard-bound book to protect the binding

edition All the copies of a work produced from the same original

edition statement The part of the description which indicates the particular edition of the work (e.g., revised, illustrated, student, abridged)

e-book A book published in electronic format and made available via the Internet or for use on a portable electronic device

e-journal A periodical published in electronic format, and made available via the Internet

Electronic Data Interchange EDI. The computer-to-computer transmission of business data in standard format between two organizations to exchange documents such as purchase orders, invoices, and claims

electronic publishing Making information available in electronic form, usually on the Internet

electronic resource management system A library management system focusing on managing and providing access to e-books, e-journals and other electronic resources

element In cataloging, a distinct piece of bibliographic information which forms part of an area of description

encumber The process of committing a certain sum of money to the payment of an order

end papers The papers which join the front and back cover of a book to the central section

end processing The preparation of an item for use in the library or for loan, after it has been cataloged

ephemera 1. Material of current interest that is expected to be stored for a limited time (e.g., pamphlets, clippings). 2. Material intended to be short-lived, but which is retained to reflect a period in time

exchange A way of acquiring material in return for a different set of material. Usually undertaken when libraries have difficulty acquiring material from particular countries, or when access to hard currency is a problem

explanatory reference A longer 'see' or 'see also' reference which explains when a heading or headings should be used

extent Also extent of resource. In RDA, the number and type of units and/or subunits making up a resource

field 1. Unit of information in a MARC record which corresponds to an area of description or other piece of information (e.g., access point). 2. Element of a record in a database

file-as-is File as the entry looks and not as it sounds (e.g., 'Mr' is not filed as 'Mister')

final processing The preparation of an item for use in the library or for loan, after it has been cataloged

fine A monetary penalty imposed on a user who returns library material after the due date

fixed location Arrangement of library materials in which items are shelved in a prescribed place, and new items are added at the end of the sequence

format (n) 1. Appearance of a publication—its size, paper, type, binding etc. 2. Layout or presentation of items in machine-readable form. 3. Physical type of an audiovisual resource (e.g., slide, filmstrip etc.) 4. Physical organization of a catalog (e.g., card, microfiche, online etc.) (v) 1. To arrange text and/or images on a screen to prepare it for printing. 2. To prepare a computer disc so that it can receive data

frequency Interval between issues of a serial (e.g., weekly, quarterly)

general material designation GMD. A concept in AACR2 used to describe the broad category of material to which a resource belongs (e.g., sound recording). RDA divides this concept into three elements: content type, media type and carrier type

gratis Provided free

hardback Also hardcover. Bound in cloth-covered or paper-covered boards

hold The status given to a library item in circulation and requested by another patron; the item can be put 'on hold' for the next patron

holdings Collection of a library or information agency

holdings policy A library's policy on the length of time, location, disposal etc. of library material, especially serials

identifier In RDA, a string of characters used to uniquely identify a resource (e.g., an ISBN, a URL) or to identify a person, family or corporate body associated with a resource

index 1. An alphabetical list of terms or topics in a resource, usually found at the back. 2. A systematically arranged list that indicates the contents of a document or group of documents

indicator In a MARC record, a character that gives additional information about a field (e.g., the first indicator 1 added to the tag 245 shows that a title added entry is to be made)

information agency An organization that provides access to information (e.g., a library, an archive)

information retrieval Finding information in a library or collection

information technology The acquisition, processing, storage and dissemination of information using computers and telecommunications

in print Available for purchase from the publisher

integrated library management system Integrated library system, ILMS, ILS. An automated package of library services that contains several functions such as circulation, cataloging etc.

integrated shelving Shelving in which all physical formats of material are shelved in one sequence

interlibrary loan ILL. A loan made by one library to another for the use of an individual, including the provision of a photocopy of the original work requested

International Standard Bibliographic Description ISBD. Standard set of bibliographic elements in standard order and with standard punctuation, published by the International Federation of Library Associations and Institutions (IFLA)

International Standard Book Number ISBN. A number intended to be unique, assigned by an agency in each country to all books published. Identifies the publisher, language and title

International Standard Serial Number ISSN. An internationally recognized number assigned to each serial publication by the International Serials Data System (ISDS), a network of national centers sponsored by Unesco

inventory 1. Also stocktaking. Checking the items in the collection, including items on loan, awaiting repair etc., against the complete record of a library's holdings (shelflist). 2. Checking library property such as furniture, stationery and equipment against a register to identify missing items. 3. The list itself

invoice A document that a dealer sends to a purchaser, itemizing the order and the amount owed

issue (n) A single copy of a serial title. (v) To lend an item

issue date The specific year and/or date, month or season by which a particular issue of a serial is identified (e.g., Spring 2014)

joint author A writer who collaborates with one or more others in the preparation of a work

journal A periodical issued by an institution, corporation or learned society containing current information and reports of activities or works in a particular field. Also used as a synonym for periodical

kick stool A library stool designed to roll along easily but lock in position when someone stands or sits on it

kit An item containing more than one kind of material, none of which is predominant (e.g., a set of slides and an audiocassette)

large-print Materials that are produced in larger than usual print (e.g., materials for the visually impaired and beginning readers, children's picture books)

lease A regular payment issued for access to online material for a period of time. The terms of the lease (how many simultaneous users per title, amount that may be downloaded or printed, etc.) are negotiated with the vendor or publisher.

letter-by-letter alphabetization Arranging in strict alphabetical order ignoring word breaks (e.g., Newbery before New England)

librarian A person with a library qualification recognized as professional by the relevant library association, or performing work at a professional level

library consortium Library network. A group of libraries joined by formal or informal agreement to achieve a specific purpose (e.g., to share the cost and use of a library management system). The consortium is often empowered to represent its members as a legal entity

Library of Congress Classification A classification scheme developed by the Library of Congress, using numbers and letters

Library of Congress Subject Headings The authoritative list of subject headings compiled and maintained by the Library of Congress

library officer Designation for a library paraprofessional, used in some countries for those with less training than a library technician and in other countries as a synonymous term

library science The study of libraries and information agencies, the role they play in society, their procedures, their history and future development

library supplier Library vendor. A company whose primary function is to supply library materials from publishers

library technician 1. A person with a qualification in librarianship recognized as paraprofessional by the relevant library association, or performing work at a paraprofessional level

licensing agreement A contract between a library and a supplier to lease databases or other resources under specific conditions for a stated period on payment of a fee

loan A recorded transaction in which a borrower removes an item from a collection for a stated period of time

location Where an item is housed. This can be the name of the library or the part of a collection

location symbol A symbol showing in which collection an item belongs (e.g., F for fiction)

loose-leaf publication A serial publication in a binder, which is kept up-to-date by inserting new pages and removing old ones according to instructions from the publisher

magazine 1. A popular periodical. 2. A holder for slides to be shown using a slide projector. Can also be used to store slides

manuscript A hand-written or typescript document

map A representation, normally to scale, of an area of the earth's surface or another celestial body

MARC Machine readable cataloging. An internationally accepted standard developed by the Library of Congress in 1966 to enable libraries to share catalog records

microfiche A microfilmed transparency about the size and shape of a filing card that can accommodate many pages of print

microfilm 16mm or 35mm wide film containing a sequence of microphotographs

microform Any form of microreproduction, including microfilm and microfiche, commonly used to preserve and store information in libraries because of its compact size

monograph A publication either complete in one part or in a finite number of separate parts

monographic series A series of related monographs with a collective title as well as individual titles

monograph in series A resource with its own title proper, that is part of a series with a common series title

name authority file A collection of authority records containing the preferred forms of headings for names, including personal and corporate names. It can be on cards, microfiche or online

national bibliography A listing of the publications of a country, about a country, by the residents of a country

national library A library maintained by government funds and serving the nation as whole. It is usually the country's legal deposit library, and collects and preserves the nation's literature

national union catalog A listing of the holdings of a large number of libraries in a country

network A system of physically separate computers with telecommunications links that allow the transfer of data among them

newspaper A printed publication issued regularly, usually daily or weekly, containing news, comment, features and advertising

non-book material Material other than printed materials (e.g., audiovisual material, computer software)

noncirculating Materials available for use within the library, but which may not be borrowed

non-fiction Books based on factual information

notation In library classification, the symbols that stand for the classes, subclasses, divisions and subdivisions of classes

note In cataloging, descriptive information that cannot be fitted into other areas of the bibliographic description

numeric designation Numbering of a serial in numeric and/or alphabetic form (e.g., Volume 1, number 1)

OH&S Occupational health and safety. Legal requirements for ensuring a 'safe' workplace

online public access catalog OPAC. A library's computer-based catalog, often including other information such as special collections, patron information, and online services or databases; usually part of an integrated library system (ILS) allowing staff from different departments to share files

on order file A listing of all the items ordered by a library and not yet received

open access Where users have direct access to items in the collection

order number The number on an order when it is placed with a supplier, which allows identification of orders without repeating bibliographic information

orders complete file A listing of orders which have been processed; includes cataloged items and cancelled orders

original cataloging Cataloging done for the first time, using cataloging tools to create the record

other title information Title on an item other than the title proper or parallel or series title; also any phrase appearing in conjunction with the title proper

out-of-print No longer available from the publisher for purchase

overdue Kept beyond the due date

ownership mark A mark indicating which library owns a particular item. It may be made with a rubber-stamp or an embossing machine or may be hand-written

pagination The number of pages or leaves (or both) of a book identified in the bibliographic description of a book

pamphlet A small (usually less than fifty pages) printed resource on a topic of current interest

pamphlet box A box usually made of cardboard, plastic or metal that is used to store pamphlets and unbound serials

paperback A book bound in flexible heavy paper or cardboard covers

parallel title Title proper in another language and/or script

patron record The record in an electronic circulation system that includes information about a borrower (e.g., name, telephone number, items on loan, holds)

periodical A serial with a distinctive title intended to appear in successive parts at stated and regular intervals. Often used as a synonym for serial and journal

period order An order from a supplier for items up to a certain total cost, without specifying particular titles

permanent loan An agreement between a library and a user for the user to retain the item 'permanently', unless it is requested by another user

physical description In AACR2, information about the physical form of an item (e.g., pagination, type of recording, dimensions)

physical processing Final processing, end processing. The preparation of an item, after it has been cataloged, for use in the library or for loan. This can include affixing library stamps, barcodes, call number labels, dust covers, etc.

preservation Changing the state of library material in order to protect the content (e.g., microfilming newspapers, digitizing slides)

process To prepare an item for use in the library or for loan; involves adding an ownership stamp, tattle tape, call number label, etc.

public library A library funded by government which provides library services to all sections of the community

public services client services, reader services. Direct services to library users, including circulation, interlibrary loan, bibliographic instruction, and reference services

publisher A person or body issuing copies of a book or other item to the public

purchase order An order placed with a supplier, usually by a government department or agency, that indicates a firm intention to purchase

reader education Helping people to derive the most benefit from using the library

realia Three-dimensional objects

recall (n) 1. A request for the return from loan of a library item. 2. Retrieval of information from a database. (v) To request the return from loan of a library item

reciprocal borrowing The exchange of borrowing privileges between two libraries

record (n) 1. A document. 2. The data relating to a document (e.g., in a catalog or database). (v) 1. To preserve information in writing, typescript or coded form. 2. To reproduce sound and/or pictures using disc or magnetic tape

reference A direction from one access point or heading to another

reference collection A collection of books intended to be referred to rather than read. Usually not for loan outside the library

relative location Library items shelved in relation to others depending on the subject

renew To extend the period for which a library item is on loan. 2. To extend the length of a serial subscription

reprint A new printing of a resource made from the original type face

reserve To request an item as soon as it is returned from loan or otherwise made ready for borrowing

reserve collection Short loan. A collection of material in high demand, usually in a teaching institution, with controlled access and shorter than normal loan periods

reshelve To replace items on the shelf in order

Resource Description and Access RDA. Descriptive cataloging guidelines replacing the Anglo-American Cataloguing Rules (AACR2), for use by libraries and other cultural collecting organizations. Released in 2010 and implemented by major collections beginning in 2013

revision A new edition of a resource containing alterations and/or additions

RFID Radio frequency identification. Technology in which clients pass their library card over a self-checking unit to register their borrower details

RT Related term. A subject heading at the same level of specificity as another heading and related in subject matter

running number A number added in the order in which the item has been received or processed

sample stocktake Checking a sample of the collection against the record of the library's holdings (e.g., checking every 100th book)

scanner A device which converts images on paper to electronic impulses readable by a computer (e.g. barcode scanner, optical scanner)

school library A library in a school which offers a library service to students and staff

see also reference A direction from one heading to another when both are used. In cataloging, RDA uses the term 'authorized access point'

see reference A direction from one heading, which is not used to another heading which is used. In cataloging, RDA uses the term 'variant access point'

segregated shelving The different formats of library materials are shelved separately according to their needs

selection The process of deciding which items to add to a library's collection

serial A publication issued in successive parts and intended to be continued indefinitely

serial issue A single copy of a serial title

serial title The title of all issues of a serial. Some serials also give titles to individual issues

serials control The process of managing the receipt, check-in, routing, and claiming of serials

series A number of works related to each other by the fact that they have a collective title, as well as each work having its own title proper

series title The collective title of a group of monographs or other resources, each of which also has an individual title

series title page In monographic series, an added title page in each monograph bearing the series title and sometimes a list of all the works in the series

shelf guide A sign to show the sequence of call numbers on a particular set of shelves

shelflist A record of the books and other resources in a library in the order in which they are shelved

shelf read To check the order of the materials on the shelves

shelve To place material in order on the shelves

software Computer program that tells the computer what to do and how to do it

sound recording A generic term for a recording of sound; available in a number of formats that include audiocassette, phonograph or vinyl record, and compact disc (digital)

special collection A collection of materials that is treated in a special way because of its subject matter, age, value, etc.

special library A library specializing in a limited subject area. Usually maintained by a corporation, association or government agency

spine label A label which is stuck on the spine of library materials showing the call number

stacks 1. The rows of shelves containing a library's collection. 2. An area containing seldom-used library materials, usually accessible only to library staff

standard number An ISBN, ISSN or any other internationally agreed upon standard number that identifies the item uniquely

standing order An order for all future issues of a serial title until the publisher is notified that no more issues are required

state library The government-funded library of a state or territory that aims to provide library services to the whole state, including support of public libraries

statement of responsibility A statement that identifies the person(s), family(ies) or corporate body(ies) responsible for the intellectual or artistic content of a resource

streaming media Video or audio content sent in compressed form over the Internet and played immediately, rather than being saved to the hard drive

subfield 1. Part of the MARC record that contains an element of description or other small piece of information. 2. Part of a field

subfield delimiter The character used to introduce a subfield in a MARC record (e.g., $)

subject cataloging Describing the content of a resource using subject headings and a classification number

subject heading A heading that describes a subject and provides subject access to a catalog

subscription An order for all issues of a periodical published within a certain time, usually one or two years. Payment is made in advance for the whole period

subscription agent A person or company which provides services to libraries wanting to purchase serials. The services include ordering subscriptions and standing orders, arranging payments and invoicing the library, following up missing issues etc.

supplement 1. An item issued separately which brings a monograph up-to-date or otherwise adds to the work. 2. Extra issues of a serial title

supplier A company whose primary function is to obtain material from publishers and supply it to information agencies

tag A label that identifies each field of a MARC record (e.g., 245 identifies the title and statement of responsibility field)

tattle tape Magnetic tape inserted in a library item that activates an alarm if the item is removed from the library without being checked out

technical services Library services that deal with the bibliographic control of library material (including acquisitions, cataloging and final processing)

terms of availability Terms on which an item is available, including price or other statement

thesaurus 1. A work containing synonymous and related words and phrases. 2. A list of controlled terms used in a database

title page The page in a printed resource that provides the most complete information about the author and title, and is used as a primary source of cataloging data

title proper The main name of an item, including alternative title/s but excluding parallel titles and other title information

UF Used For. A term to introduce a non-preferred term for a subject or name, to refer users to a preferred term

uniform title An AACR2 cataloging concept, with different definitions for monographs and serials. RDA uses 'preferred title of a work' as a similar, but not exactly equivalent concept. 1. In AACR2 cataloging, a title chosen to identify a monograph appearing under varying titles (e.g., Bible). 2. In AACR2 cataloging, a title used to distinguish the heading for one serial or series from the heading for another serial or series (e.g., Bulletin (UNESCO))

union catalog Catalog of the holdings of more than one library

unique call number A number on a library item consisting of a classification number, a book number (or Cutter number) and often a location symbol, which is different from every other call number in the library

variant access point In RDA cataloging, a non-preferred variation of a title or name. Known as a 'see reference' in AACR2, it provides a direction from an access point that is not used to an authorized access point that is used

variant title A different form of the title

vendor A company that provides serials, supplies, library systems, databases, and other products and services for a fee

verification Checking data to confirm bibliographic details

version A different edition, manifestation or adaptation of a work

verso The left-hand page of an open book; the back of a leaf of a book (e.g., verso of the title page)

vertical file A collection of ephemeral material including pamphlets and newspaper clippings. Usually arranged in subject order in a filing cabinet

videotape Strip of mylar plastic tape covered with iron oxide which can be magnetized. Sound and pictures are encoded as magnetic signals

vinyl record A sound disc made of vinyl plastic, with sound grooves pressed into the surface

volume 1. What is contained in one binding of a monograph. 2. A number of issues of a serial, usually those published in one twelve-month period

weed, weeding Also deselection. Discarding resources that are considered to be of no further use to the library, and removing their catalog records

word-by-word alphabetization Arranging in strict alphabetical order within each word (e.g., New Town before newness)

World Wide Web A collection of sites on the Internet in which users can move easily from one document or site to another by means of hypertext links

Z39.50 A client/server-based information retrieval protocol for library applications, designed to aid retrieval from distributed servers. Issued by the American National Standards Institute/National Information Standards Organization (ANSI/NISO Z39.50)

BIBLIOGRAPHY

A step-by-step guide to keeping your books alive. Knoxfield, Vic: Raeco, [1996].

Black, Steve. *Serials in libraries: issues and practices*. Westport, CT: Libraries Unlimited, 2006.

Evans, G. Edward, Intner, Sheila S and Weihs, Jean. Introduction to technical services. Westport, CT: Libraries Unlimited, 2010.

Farkas, Lynn and Rowe, Helen. *Learn cataloging the RDA way.* International edition. Friendswood, Tex: TotalRecall Publications, Inc., 2015.

Ganedran, Jacinta. *Learn library management.* International edition. Friendswood, Tex: TotalRecall Publications, Inc., 2015.

Guidelines for best practice in interlibrary loan and document delivery. IFLA. Last revised 2007. http://www.ifla.org/publications/guidelines-for-best-practice-in-interlibrary-loan-and-document-delivery. (viewed November 2014)

Harvey, Ross and Mahard, Martha R. *The preservation management handbook: a twenty-first century guide for libraries, archives and museums.* Lanham, MD: Rowman & Littlefield, 2014.

Harvey, Ross. *Preserving digital materials*. 2nd ed. Berlin: De Gruyter Saur, 2011.

Rowe, Helen. *Learn about information.* International edition. Friendswood, Tex: TotalRecall Publications, Inc., 2015.

Totterdell, Anne. *An introduction to library and information work*. London: Facet Publishing, 2005.

Weingand, Darlene E. *Customer service excellence: a concise guide for librarians*. Chicago, Ill.: American Library Association, 1997.

INDEX

CPSIA information can be obtained
at www.ICGtesting.com
Printed in the USA
LVHW060529200722
723872LV00002B/19

9 781590 954348